SOCIAL LIFE IN VIRGINIA
During the War for Independence

Colonel Landon Carter (1710-1778) of Sabine Hall, Richmond County. Attributed to Charles Bridges. T. Dabney Wellford, and R. Carter Wellford, owners. *Courtesy of Virginia Historical Society.*

SOCIAL LIFE IN VIRGINIA
During the War for Independence

By Elizabeth Cometti
Professor of History, Emeritus
West Virginia University

Edward M. Riley, *Editor*

Published by the

Virginia Independence Bicentennial Commission

Box JF

Williamsburg, Virginia 23185

Commonwealth of Virginia
Virginia Independence Bicentennial Commission

Lewis A. McMurran, Jr., *Chairman*
Hunter B. Andrews, *Vice Chairman*

Fred W. Bateman
Garland Gray
Omer Lee Hirst
John Warren Cooke
W. C. Daniel
Frank E. Mann
Sam E. Pope
John Sears, Jr.

Robert R. Gwathmey III
A. E. Dick Howard
W. Moscoe Huntley
E. M. Hutton
Mrs. Carolyn Moses Lusardi
Mrs. Perry W. Moore
Jack C. Smith
John C. Stephens, Jr.

Parke Rouse, Jr., *Director*
Robert L. Scribner, *Historian*

Committee on Publications
Edward M. Riley,
Chairman

Francis L. Berkeley, Jr.
Alf J. Mapp, Jr.
A. E. Dick Howard

John M. Jennings
William F. Swindler
Louis H. Manarin

George H. Reese

I.

VIRGINIA society of the Revolutionary War period was conspicuous for its class distinctions. Its stratifications belied the egalitarianism expressed in the Declaration of Independence and the Virginia Declaration of Rights. Ebenezer Hazard, a visitor from Pennsylvania, observed, "There is much greater Disparity between the Rich & the Poor in Virginia than in any of the Northern States"; and the differences were not confined to material possessions. Class-conscious foreigners who came to Virginia during the Revolution were most explicit on this score. The Englishman Thomas Anburey discerned three ranks of white people in addition to that of the enslaved blacks. The first class, which was composed of the "best" families in respect to lineage, fortune, and education, moved with sophisticated, self-assured ease among their peers. The second and most numerous class was not so easily identifiable because of social and economic variations among its members; in general, though, they were regarded as "valuable members of the community" and not deficient in intellectual faculties. The third class was smaller in Virginia than in other areas. Many of this class were transported felons. Rude, illiberal, noisy, turbulent were the disparaging labels attached to these people. They were impertinently curious, lazy, immoral, and extremely belligerent and revengeful when drunk; their fights made English boxing matches seem like exercises in humanity.

Poverty and slavery in the midst of conspicuous opulence shocked most the Frenchman Marquis de Chastellux: "It is in this state, for the first time since I crossed the sea, that I have seen poor people. For, among these rich plantations where the Negro alone is wretched, one often finds miserable huts inhabited by whites, whose wan looks and

1

ragged garments bespeak poverty." The cause of the poor whites' depressed status was the concentration of land in the hands of a few men who, although owning thousands of acres—Landon Carter had nearly 50,000 acres—utilized only as much as their slaves could cultivate and refused to dispose of any of it.

The first families of Virginia were a fascinating lot, displaying, with rare exceptions, common virtues and foibles. Through social exclusiveness and intermarriage they formed an elitist society that was hard for the upstart to penetrate. "The very basis of the gentleman's status was the recognition of an inherent inequality in mankind," Louis Wright has observed. A gentleman was wealthy—he had to be in order to act like one and receive proper respect. "Who is he?" and "what is he worth?" were not improper inquiries to make of a stranger among the Virginia gentry. A gentleman watched his manners—at least outside the home—though within turbulence might prevail. A gentleman adhered to a code of conduct based on truth and honor, but he condoned the sins of the flesh and the unbridled tongue, particularly in the use of profanity. Learning, based chiefly on the humanities, was a mark of gentility and was rightly held in higher esteem than the coats of arms which Virginia descendants of London merchants and tradesmen aspired to. Despite his passionate attachment to horses (though Carter vowed that "to give a young man a horse is to make him an ass") and his luxurious tastes, a gentleman seriously attended to his many and varied responsibilities like a true *pater familias*. In matters of religion a gentleman was tolerant to the point of indifference and very practical in church administration.

The innate graciousness of the Virginia gentleman shone brilliantly during the Revolution toward enemy prisoners and Gallic-Catholic allies—officers, of course, and peers—who came to the state. While Baron de Riedesel, commander of the Brunswick troops who surrendered at Saratoga, resided with his lovely wife and little daughters at Colle, he received many courtesies from his neighbor at Monticello, Thomas Jefferson. Jefferson's conduct was not unique. Indeed, so generous were the Virginia aristocrats in this respect that they were occasionally charged with being pro-British. But with the self-assurance born of position and wealth they shrugged their shoulders at such criticism and continued to extend hospitality as they pleased, to grant special favors to their former enemies, to refrain from embarrassing them by discussing politics, and to avoid censoring their mail. For this kind of liberality, reported Anburey,

Major General Chevalier de Chastellux (1734-1788) at age forty-eight by
Charles Willson Peale. *Courtesy of Independence National Historical Park
Collection.*

neighbors of Colonel Thomas Mann Randolph threatened to set fire to his mills, whereupon at the next court day the intrepid Colonel warned that no one had "a right to scrutinize into his private concerns," especially since his public character was well known. To emphasize his point he offered £500 for the identity of his menacers and was more attentive than ever to the British officers. In general the French allies lived on "good terms" with the Virginians. Although it was well known that Americans did not "waste kisses on men" when they bade adieus, leave-taking with the French was sometimes done in both the French manner, that is kissing the cheeks, and the American manner, shaking hands.

The owners of middling plantations undoubtedly shared some of the characteristics of their social and economic betters. Many of these lesser planters, like those more affluent, employed overseers, although they could have attended to plantation affairs themselves. Lack of interest and training in cultural refinements and a combination of laziness and contempt for work because it was regarded as demeaning, sometimes led to corrosive idleness.

The "lower" sort—inquisitive, suspicious, and ignorant— constituted a "lawless set" marked by a "ferocious disposition." A group of these ruffians once attempted to kill or castrate a poor British officer because he had innocently aroused the jealousy of a husband from whose wife he had been buying poultry and milk. When drunk—and this happened often—these men might turn an innocuous argument into a savage brawl with no holds barred. Their living quarters were occasionally downright repellent—fetid, vermin-infested and filthy. "What a pity it is," exclaimed Anburey, "that a country where the superior class are such a hospitable and friendly disposition, should be rendered almost unsafe to live in by the barbarity of the [common] people."

On the frontier, class distinctions disappeared before the ever-present danger of Indian attack. Some found the pioneers utterly antipathetic—insubordinate, undisciplined, and crude. Yet they were capable of outstanding acts of heroism, of enduring the hardships of taking refuge in a fort, of rendering assistance to others—in short, of deserving their legendary reputation, which they helped to create, by being "very taleful of the Indian Wars."

Hospitality was, with rare exception, a common virtue in Virginia. "If a stranger went amonst them, no matter of what country," recorded Nicholas Cresswell, who was in Virginia for three years, "if he behaved decently, had a good face, a good coat and a tolerable share of good-nature, would dance with the women and drink with the men, with a little necessary adulation—of which, by the way, they are very fond—with these qualifications he would be entertained amongst them with greatest friendship as long as he pleased to stay." Only rarely did one encounter an exception. A traveler in Virginia was welcome to help himself to the fruit growing near the road; moreover, if the owner of the orchard saw him taking the fruit, he would direct the traveler to the tree that bore the best fruit. Colonel Archibald Cary of Ampthill was even importunate toward his guests. "By God you shall dine with me today," he is supposed to have said to General Nathanael Greene.

What effect the Revolution had in obscuring, if not obliterating, class lines is difficult to determine. It appeared to Anburey that before the war "the spirit of equality or leveling principal was not so prevalent in Virginia, as in the other provinces; and that the different classes of people in the former supported a greater distinction than those of the latter; . . . " But the war modified this situation. In proof, the Englishman recounted that on a visit to Colonel Randolph three "country peasants" who had come to Tuckahoe on business entered the room where the family was sitting and proceeded to make themselves comfortable by the fire, spitting and taking off their muddy boots. When they had gone, someone commented on the liberties they had taken, to which Randolph replied that it was "unavoidable, the spirit of independency was converted into equality, and every one who bore arms, esteemed himself upon a footing with his neighbour," including the Colonel himself. Even before the adoption of the Declaration of Independence Landon Carter noted some of this spirit. A small planter in Richmond County, solicited to lend assistance against a British tender, "asked the People if they were such fools to go to protect the Gentlemen's houses on the river side; he thought it would be better if they were burnt down." More alarming than what was said on this occasion, though, was the fact that the local revolutionary committee, composed of new men, took no notice of it. "Hurray for Independancy, Sedition, and Confusion," exploded the master of Sabine Hall. By 1777 Carter's disillusionment was complete: "The Election day, to which I shall not go nor ever I beleive again; for verily our salt has lost its savoryness; . . . " This may have been true on the local level of government, but not in the exclusive top echelons.

Far beneath the poor whites were the slaves, ill-lodged, ill-fed, ill-clothed, overwhelmed with work, dehumanized by their legal status as property, and frequently subjected to shameful abuse. Although Jefferson labelled the treatment of slaves in Virginia as "mild," both American and foreign visitors thought it generally otherwise. On learning that the weekly food allowance of the blacks at Nomini Hall was only a peck of corn and a pound of meat a head and that Robert Carter was yet considered a humane master, Philip Vickers Fithian exclaimed: "Good God! are these Christians?" On some plantations the cruel method of extracting obedience may have accounted for the large number of runaways during the American Revolution. To some extent the overseers, "unfeeling monsters," Anburey called them, were responsible for the treatment of slaves except those who served as domestics. And yet the masters were responsible for the choice of overseers.

Foreigners were even more repelled than northerners by slavery. "In general, despotism and aristocracy are the rule in Virginia more than elsewhere," wrote Baron von Closen. "A beagle, a *lap-dog*, very often leads a happier life and is much better fed than the poor negroes or mulattoes, who have only their allowance of corn daily with which to do as they please. They have salt meat only once a week. That is the way these miserable beings live. It is true that they recoup themselves often with their light-fingered hands and pilfer some victuals, even money, with incredible dexterity." But this was risky business, for the standard punishment for petty offenses was 39 lashes, probably well laid on, and for more serious thievery the culprit was branded in the hand and given an additional 39 lashes.

But there were also enlightened Virginians of both sexes who were responsive to the basic needs of their slaves, particularly on the score of health, though it might be argued that this was a matter of self-interest, of preservation of property. Even a stern master like Landon Carter, who did not hesitate to whip his blacks for idleness, for attempting to run away, or, in the case of a woman, for "sallatiousness," tenderly imposed his questionable medical skill on a faithful old slave, Jack Lubbar, once a foreman on the Carter plantation. Richard Henry Lee, in considering the advisability of disposing of much of his property because of rising inflation and investing the returns in six percent Continental bonds, saw only one objection, namely, "the parting with Negroes, upon principles of humanity," although he thought that a few of the oldest and best

Tuckahoe, Goochland County. Built about 1712 by Thomas Randolph (1689-1730) and enlarged after the builder's death in 1730. *Courtesy of Colonial Williamsburg Foundation.*

might be retained and placed in good families until they would again be needed.

Although the Virginia Declaration of Rights of June 1776 proclaimed that "all men are by nature equally free and independent, and have certain inherent rights . . . namely, the enjoyment of life and liberty, with the means of acquiring and possessing property, and pursuing and obtaining happiness and safety," it was obvious that this exalted affirmation did not apply to the slaves. But it must have pricked many a Virginia conscience. Only two important legislative measures affecting slavery were enacted in Virginia during the Revolution. The first, passed in 1778, terminated the importation of slaves in Virginia by sea or land and further provided that any slave imported in violation of the act should be free; but a person from any of the United States might remove to Virginia with his slaves, provided they had not been imported from Africa or any of the West Indies since November 1, 1778. Inasmuch as colonial Virginia had attempted without success to check the importation of blacks through the imposition of an import tax, the Act of 1778 did not reflect a purging of the mind on slavery, nor did it benefit those already in bondage. The second measure, passed in 1782, was more humanitarian since it made it lawful for any person by testamentary action or other instrument in writing scaled and witnessed to manumit his slave or slaves. The effect of this law is indicated by the yearly manumissions which averaged over 1,000 for the next ten years. Moreover it stimulated subsequent liberalization of manumission law.

Actually it was neither law nor an increasing awareness of the discrepancy between revolutionary ideology and slavery that brought freedom to thousands of blacks, but, rather, British promises of liberation, for those who had the courage to escape to British lines. Thus, John Murray, Earl of Dunmore, the last royal governor of Colonial Virginia, may well deserve to be acclaimed as "liberator" through the issuance of his proclamation promising freedom to indentured servants, blacks, and others who were willing to bear arms for the British. Those who responded to this and subsequent calls to liberation, real or imagined, were the young, the capable, the skilled, the fearless, and the resourceful. The British used blacks in the land and naval forces—on foraging and impressment expeditions they were particularly useful—and as informers, pilots, construction workers, military servants, and jacks-of-all-trades.

Blacks, either privately or state owned, as well as free, were used in

Virginia in manufacturing, mining, transportation and manning the small state navy, which contained nearly 150 black seamen, one out of ten of whom was free. Some of these men rendered able service as pilots and participated creditably in several naval engagements, for which they occasionally received their freedom. When the Virginia Council in November 1782 called for 3,500 men to level the works at Yorktown and at the same time permitted the draftees to present free blacks as substitutes, some masters sent their slaves, promising them freedom. On the discharge of the latter, a number of former owners tried to reenslave them, but Governor Benjamin Harrison prevented this shameful repudiation of so vital a pledge, and the legislature ordered that slaves who had served should be free.

The American Revolution improved the lot of the black only to the extent that it increased the narrow paths to freedom, and, as Jefferson hoped, may have started "ripening" of minds of Virginians "for a complete emancipation of human nature," a large order, indeed. Even a humanitarian like Jefferson, who regarded slavery as a "great political and moral evil," retained his slaves, along with the conviction that they were physically and intellectually inferior to the Caucasians. Although the ideology of 1776 may have pricked some private consciences, it produced no public outcry against slavery, no systematic effort to end it, and no apologia for it.

II.

"THE reigning spirit in Virginia is liberty—and the universal topic politicks—" Philip Fithian told Pelatiah Webster in August 1774. This was true. Virginians applauded the resistance to the Tea Act of 1773 and forbore drinking the politically obnoxious weed, taking, instead coffee when they could afford it. Virginia answered the call to participate in the First Continental Congress at Philadelphia by sending some of her most distinguished sons, one of whom, Peyton Randolph, an affable aristocrat of "majestic deportment," was chosen president of the patriotic assembly. And it was a Virginia delegate, Patrick Henry, who announced to that body that the "Distinctions between Virginians, Pennsylvanians, New Yorkers, and New Englanders, are no more. I am not a Virginian, but an American."

The most important achievement of the First Continental Congress was the adoption of the much-debated Association. It provided for non-importation of British goods and slaves, for the discontinuance of the slave trade, for deferred non-exportation, and for improving sheep breeding. Article VIII was a blockbuster for the sociable Virginians, as it prohibited horse-racing, gaming, theatrical performances, and other "expensive" forms of entertainment; and some mourning practices, such as the giving of scarves and gloves at funerals, were to be discontinued.

Virginians of all classes and ages were passionate devotees of horse-racing. Most towns of any size held races, especially at fair time, with purses ranging from a few to several hundred pounds; and near the ordinaries in the interior parts of the province one usually saw two paths about six or eight feet apart and a quarter of a mile in length for quarter-racing. Prominent Virginians like Colonel John Tayloe of Mount Airy owned race horses which were ridden by boys before

Peyton Randolph (c. 1721-1775) by Charles Willson Peale. *Courtesy of Independence National Historical Park Collection.*

many fans. In one race at Richmond County Court House (now Warsaw) the horses covered the one-mile course in two minutes, but slowed down by the fifth time around. Williamsburg had an excellent course for two-, three-, or four-mile heats, where races that generally lasted a week were run every spring and fall for purses raised by subscription. The horses that participated, observed Anburey, "would make no contemptible figure at Newmarket." Quarter-racing, a match between two horses running a quarter of a mile, was a favorite diversion of the middling and lower classes, whose horses were trained to get into full speed at the start and maintain their velocity to the end. Since these races were quickly terminated, they were sometimes followed by barbarous boxing matches between "buckskins," the epithet given to the Virginians by New Englanders in retaliation for their being called Yankees.

Virginians never tired of talking about horses, particularly their own horses, and probably more than one teen-age scion of a prominent family had no higher goal than to be an efficient groom. So much did Virginians prize their blue-blooded horses that in the inflationary year of 1780 Colonel Thomas Randolph offered $1,000 for the delivery of a horse that had been stolen and $2,000 "on Conviction of the thief," provided he were executed. During his visit to Richmond at the end of the Revolution, Dr. Johann Schoepf noted that government business brought so many gentlemen there with their fine horses, that the young capital resembled "an Arabian village." All day long one saw "saddled horses at every turn, and a swarming of riders in the few and muddy streets, for a horse must be mounted, if only to fetch a prise of snuff from across the way . . . . Horses are a prime object with the Virginians . . . ."

Two months before the meeting of the First Continental Congres, this card appeared in the *Virginia Gazette*: "A Virginian presents his compliments to the JOCKEY CLUBS of Fredericksburg and Portsmouth, and begs that they will suppress their sporting spirit till the circumstances of America can permit it with more decency. He also begs leave to recommend it to the serious consideration of these clubs whether their purses, applied to the relief of the distressed *BOSTONIANS*, would not afford them more real pleasure than all that can arise from viewing a painful contest between two or three animals." Fine sentiments indeed, but they fell on deaf ears. Off to the races went the gentry, and doubtless the middling and lower sort did likewise. If the Association had any effect on the suppressing of racing it was only brief—and very desultory—despite the decline in the number of advertisements of races and the example set by the Dumfries Jockey Club in postponing its fall races in 1774. The British prisoners of war interned in Virginia in 1779 witnessed the two favorite types of races; so did the French allies who were in the state prior to and after the siege of Yorktown; and, most important, so did the Virginians, though they did not shout the fact to the press. It would take more than a war to suppress one of Virginia's favorite sports.

In his intimate and outspoken diary, Colonel Landon Carter of Sabine Hall laid bare his suffering at the hands of his son Robert, a man of abrasive character and incurably addicted to gambling and its attendant vices. "I don't know a worse man than a devoted gamester; and no man who is so should ever marry; for the married gamester keeps his family in the Perpetual fear of starving," wrote the heartbroken old man on seeing his feckless son at the card table day after day from morning until bedtime. "Good God," he groaned, "that such a monster had descended from my loins." And shortly before he died, the Colonel offered another strong argument against gaming, namely, the use of false dice by professional gamblers, a practice which almost involved his grandson in a duel.

Responsible Virginians, of course, had long been concerned about the pervasive gambling problem that had led some men, among them William Byrd III, to suicide. Even the professors of William and Mary College, who should have set a good example, were known to play cards all night in Williamsburg's public houses. In 1752 Governor Robert Dinwiddie had urged the discouragement of "Gaming, Swearing, and immoderate drinking, particularly at the County Courts." The first of these crimes, he had contended, was "pretty general in this Country, and [was] now much practiced among the lower Class of . . . People: . . Tradesmen, and inferior planters, who in all Countries [were] very apt to follow the Examples of their Superiors." This "great Vice" was "often attended with many other Sins, and frequently with the ruin of families." To emphasize his point Dinwiddie had asked all magistrates to enforce the anti-gaming laws.

In truth, if the "Act for preventing excessive and deceitful Gaming" passed in 1748 had been executed, betting at cards, dice, tennis, bowls, horse-racing, and cock-fighting in public or private places would have disappeared, and the "divers lewd and dissolute persons" who lived "at great expenses, having no visible estate, profession, or calling, to support them, but by gaming only" would have been effectively put out of business. For the laws voided gambling debts and provided: (1) that real estate encumbered by gambling should devolve to the next heir; (2) that the loser of forty shillings or more could recover all money paid in gambling; (3) that ordinary keepers who permitted gambling on their premises would be fined; (4) that cheats would forfeit five times the value of the money won at cards, would be deemed "infamous," and would suffer such corporal punishment as in cases of willful perjury; (5) and that persons provoking fights as a result of gambling would be fined and rendered liable to prosecution at common law.

Although "excessive and deceitful" gambling was prohibited, the playing of games as such was not, and the act specifically permitted billiards, bowls, backgammon, chess, or draughts to be played at public places. In the mansions of Virginia both men and women enjoyed card games. One of the most popular of these was whist, a predecessor of bridge, usually played by four persons, two against two, with fifty-two cards. Both Martha Washington and Martha Jefferson were whist enthusiasts and occasionally lost a little money at the game. At Virginia's favorite spa, Warm Springs, (now Berkeley Springs, West Virginia), where, despite the clouds of war there were about four hundred visitors in September 1775, popular card games were played in the dining room of the tavern: "five and forty," which somewhat resembled euchre; whist; "all-fours," a type of "high, low, jack, game," which derived its name from the four chances involved; and the now totally extinct "Callico-Betty."

Not all games were played with cards. In one called "Button," pawns could be redeemed with kisses, so it was a favorite with young people. The leading player in "Break the Pope's Neck," was, of course, the person chosen by the company to play the pope; the others players were designated "friars." What transpired in "Grind the Bottle and Hide the Thimble" was probably innocent enough, judging from its name. For those who were "Searching Houses above to know/What shall happen to them below" *The Complete Fortune Teller* was available. One could also find *Conversation Cards* ornamented with copperplate cuts and designed, so it was advertised, to amuse, as well as to improve the mind by exercising the imagination and enlarging the understanding of the players. No one could be the loser in this game.

The eighth article of the Association which forbade "all kinds of gaming" doubtless puzzled many Virginians. Taken literally the prohibition was indeed restrictive. "Is it allowable to play at any game tolerated by our laws for small sums only as an amusement?" someone very properly inquired. Since the committees charged with enforcement of the Association provided no guidelines, the prudent man should perhaps take the prohibition literally and desist altogether from playing.

Such an end to gaming, of course, did not occur, though the Congressional injunction may have produced a brief pause. By January 1775, vigilant local committees were hearing cases involving gaming. The Northumberland County Committee advertised William Lewis and Anthony McKenley because the former had won from the latter a silver watch, two pairs of leather breeches, and two men's hats. When Francis Moore was haled before the Orange County Committee for having violated the Association by gambling, he "gave such evidence of his penitence, and intention to observe the association strictly in the future" that the Committee thought it proper "to re-admit him into the number of friends to the public cause, till a second transgression" occurred.

Lest such leniency give encouragement to other gamblers, the Committee added that mitigation of the prescribed punishment proceeded only "from a desire to distinguish penitent and submissive from refractory and obstinate offenders." The Southampton Committee displayed similar forbearance by excusing four men who had coupled their admission to having gambled with a willingness to refund everything they had won. Assurance of good conduct in the future also moved the Sussex County Committee to excuse a group that had gambled in a private home. On the other hand, the Caroline County Committee advertised luckless Rodham Kenner for having gambled in his own house. Perhaps he had not been sufficiently abject in his apologies. And for a second offender, one who had enticed others into partaking of his guilt by first making them drunk, the Committee attached the dreaded label of "enemy to American liberty."

If the alarmists spoke the truth, by the spring of 1776 many vices, particularly gambling, were once more prevalent throughout Virginia. These people urged that at the next election anyone who was in the "least attached to gaming" should be thrown out of office and replaced by men of good Christian character. Voters should pay particular attention to the choice of committeemen "for what favour, or blessing" could be expected from heaven when so many in the country were "running headlong into all manner of sin and wickedness." Apparently the voters did not heed this sober advice, and gambling continued to be "amazingly prevalent" in Williamsburg, even among the legislators. The Council must have been aware of this, for it ordered the mayor and all the magistrates to use their utmost endeavors to put the anti-gambling laws into execution.

This order did not go far enough in the opinion of the self-appointed guardians of public morals who charged that "sharpers" were waylaying soldiers for their bounty money and officers for both their pay and the public money entrusted to them for recruiting troops. Such practices retarded enlistment at the very time when the country needed all the support it could get. Instead of patriotic dedication, the general public seemed to be "actuated only by the old Epicurean maxim, *Let us eat, drink, and be merry, for to-morrow we die.*" Such "melancholy" reflection must have increased when someone discovered that a package containing three packs of cards had been sent to a magistrate. How could anyone expect to have an orderly society when those who were supposed to be the "terrors" to evil-doers violated the law? Perhaps the best solution was to declare that anyone found gaming, racing, or in a similar manner violating the law should be drafted into the armed forces—not an attractive situation to many Virginians—and treated accordingly. The utility of such a law at a time when recruitment was very much in arrears would counterbalance the objection that such a drastic measure would bring odium on the military.

The Virginia censors finally had their way in the fall of 1779, when the legislature passed a comprehensive act to "suppress excessive gaming." Once again contracts for paying gambling debts were voided; again conveyances to secure money or other winnings were to inure to the benefit of the loser's heir; again tavern keepers were penalized for permitting gaming on their premises. But two provisions were new: lotteries and raffling were prohibited; and gamblers winning or losing more than five pounds in the space of twenty-four hours were rendered incapable of holding any civil office; moreover, anyone gambling in tavern, racefield, or other place of public resort was to be deemed "an infamous gambler" and was to be ineligible to any office of trust or honor in the state.

On paper, at least, the success of the censors was complete. In practice, though, such must not have been the case according to the advertisement of William Brown of Bedford County, who on two different occasions lost to "a set of sharpers with marked cards and false dice" a very considerable sum in money, horses, bonds running into the thousands of pounds, and "other things." Taking advantage of the gaming law, Brown warned the public that all the bonds listed in the notice would be disputed and that no person should take an assignment to them, as they would not be honored.

What probably checked gambling temporarily was not the severity of the law—though that might have been a factor—but the critical military situation that culminated in the American triumph at Yorktown. By the end of 1781, however, gambling was once more the rage, and again some members of the legislature were seen at the gaming table. One prominent James River planter was obliged to part with slaves, horses, and other property valued at 1008 hogsheads of tobacco in order to pay off his debts. If one could play with immunity in the capital town of Richmond, certainly no restraint could be expected in the plantation homes of the Tidewater or the mean ordinaries of the western section.

Cock-fighting, interdicted by the Association along with gambling, was a brutal sport in which trained roosters shorn of some of their feathers and armed with long steel spurs viciously attacked each other until one of the bleeding adversaries dropped in agonizing death. Revolting as was the spectacle, cock-fighting attracted rich, poor, and slaves; only foreigners were utterly repelled by it. "I was before Dinner very strongly urged, by Mr Taylor, Mr Randolph, & some others to attend a Cock-Fight, where 25 Cocks are to fight, & large Sums are betted, so large at one as twenty five Pounds," recorded Philip Fithian in 1774. At these fights the Virginia aristocrats rubbed shoulders with vagabonds living from hand to mouth by betting, as well as with more settled citizens of the "lower sort."

When a match was announced in various parts of Virginia, the news spread by word of mouth "with such facility" that spectators came from as many as forty miles away, "some with cocks, but all with money for betting." Since the ordinaries near which the cock-fights were held could not provide accommodations for all the assembled fans, each person brought his own provisons, and everyone who came from a distance slept on the floor in one large room. This barbarous sport, especially popular in the South, where fighting cocks acquired wide reputations, ran a close second to race horses as topics of manly conversation.

Only occasionally was a voice raised in protest. The will of Robert Page of Broadneck, for instance, stipulated that neither of his sons "ever be allowed to go to Horse Races or Cock Fights, or to any other public diversion" as such spectacles were only time consuming.

Undoubtedly the Association temporarily discouraged public amusements, including cock-fighting, since their promoters ran the risk of being denounced by some patriot—but only temporarily. By 1777 horse-racing and cock-fighting were again the sporting rage, with inter-county cock matches as special attractions. As the conflict for independence dragged on, more and more of the old habits, good and bad, were resumed without any qualms, for Virginians had no taste for the grey garb of austerity.

Indeed, some practices had never been discarded. Among them was eye gouging, illegal and barbarous though it was. High-born Virginians preferred the use of pistols, swords, and words to defend their honor; but the "meaner" and more conspicuously volatile sort employed every form of violence when fighting drunk—kicking, scratching, pinching, biting, tripping, and worst of all, gouging, accompanied by cursing and howling loud enough to repel the squeamish and at the same time attract an audience. To insure victory in a gouging match, some men kept the nails of the thumb and second finger excessively long and pointed and hardened them with a candle. Only when one of the antagonists called out "King's curse," the equivalent of "enough," did a fight end in time to prevent an eye from being gouged out of the socket. The matches usually took place around ordinaries, where liquor flowed freely, and at the county seats at election time. So fearful of these fights were the British prisoners of war, with whom the rabble was always trying to pick a quarrel, that they never ventured out without side-arms.

Virginia, unlike some colonies to the north, was not founded by religious dissidents bent on establishing rigidly moralistic common-wealths. This was a consequential factor in shaping Virginia's social climate, which, perhaps more than that of any other province, retained many English characteristics throughout the colonial period. Unencumbered by puritanical prejudices, Virginians zest-fully continued to enjoy many of the same diversions that had earned for the homeland the attractive appellation of Merry Old England. Some of these diversions were coarse, to say the least, but one of them, the theatre, was richly nourished by England's greatest literary genius and lesser lights, and was a favorite not only in London, but also in the English provincial towns, where charming little playhouses were constructed according to a general pattern.

The first theatre in the British colonies was constructed between 1716 and 1718 in Williamsburg on the east side of the Palace green; although in 1745 the building was converted to use as a Court of Hustings, better days for the Williamsburg theatre were ahead. In 1751 Alexander Finnie, proprietor of Raleigh Tavern, undertook to erect a playhouse in which the Murray-Kean Company, a semi-professional troupe, might perform. When Lewis Hallam in 1752 brought to Williamsburg his truly professional repertory, well equipped with costumes and scenery, he purchased and improved the theatre by finishing its interior walls so as better to insulate the house and provide acoustical aid to the performers. In the ensuing twenty years Virginia audiences saw a variety of performances, beginning with *The Merchant of Venice* and *The Anatomist*, a farce. The playhouse in Williamsburg remained until 1775; five years later the property on which it stood was sold, and by 1787 the building had disappeared, even to the brick of the foundation.

But Thespis was not completely bereft of votaries during the conflict for independence. Students of the College of William and Mary and amateur groups composed of both sexes probably continued to perform now and then; and probably exhibitions of some kind could be seen at fairs. Although the number of fairs diminished greatly—they had been held in Alexandria, Fredericksburg, Halifax County, Hanover County, Henrico County, Mecklenburg County, Newcastle, Norfolk, Richmond, Williamsburg in April and December, and even in far-off Staunton—they did not disappear altogether. Fairs were important, almost necessary, annual events inherited from England, and persons attending them were, with their possessions, exempt from arrests, attachments, and executions except for capital offenses, breaches of the peace, and controversies. Here goods were displayed, bought, and sold; bounties were given for encouraging manufacturing; land was purchased; all kinds of competitions, including horse-racing, were held; lotteries for defraying the cost of building churches and schools were drawn; and popular entertainments such as puppet shows and tightrope performances were presented at the major fairs such as the one in Fredericksburg.

Yet in these years of greatly curtailed public amusement one theatre was constructed in Virginia, the only one anywhere during the Revolution. This was a plain log hut erected in 1779 by British prisoners of war interned in Charlottesville. Might they have performed *Maid of the Oaks* written by their former commander, General John Burgoyne?

Before the War for Independence Virginians had loyally celebrated the milestones of the royal family with fireworks, illuminations, and "splendid" balls attended by the governor and his lady. After the patriots somewhat abruptly transformed George III from a respected monarch to an infamous tyrant, the course of events produced other, more politically flavored, occasions for celebrations. In July 1776, when the Declaration of Independence was proclaimed at Williamsburg, the town received the exciting news "with universal applause" punctuated by the discharge of cannon and small arms and followed by illuminations in the evening. Up the James, the burgeoning little village of Richmond celebrated in a similar fashion with nearly one thousand persons in attendance. On these patriotic occasions, thirteen toasts were in order, and these doubtless led to many others honoring the nascent state and its new heroes.

Following the Declaration of Independence Virginia and the rest of the nation had little cause for celebration until the surrender of General Burgoyne at Saratoga in October 1777. This victory inspired Virginians to protracted festivities. On October 30 came a *feu de joie* and a military parade, whose participants had been ordered to appear clean, shaved, with their hats cocked and their arms and accoutrements in good order. A gill of rum was issued to each in evidence of Governor Patrick Henry's hearty congratulations. The Governor further commemorated the great event by proclaiming November 13 as a day of thanksgiving.

What ensued must have pleased everyone in the "very crowded audience." The Reverend John Bracken of Williamsburg began with "an excellent discourse"; this was followed by an "animating sermon" delivered by the Reverend James Madison, chaplain of the General Assembly and president of the College of William and Mary. In the evening the legislators offered a "grand ball" and entertainment at the Capitol, which was attended by many ladies and gentlemen as well as military personnel and "strangers" in the town. Last, the cannon discharged thirteen salvos in honor of Washington, Horatio Gates (also a Virginian), and other heroes of the day.

The victory of Franco-American forces at Yorktown in October 1781 produced demonstrations of joy throughout the new nation, now become confident of victory. Illuminations, peans of thanksgiving, salvos and more salvos, and, of course, balls were the order of the day. On October 24, 1781, a week after the surrender of General Cornwallis, the Continental Congress went in solemn procession to the Dutch Lutheran Church to return thanks to God for crowning the allied armies with success. Later, the Congress ordered that a marble column adorned with emblems of the alliance be erected at the site of the triumph. In Williamsburg a *Te Deum* was sung on December 15, and that evening General Rochambeau gave a dinner and ball for the leading citizens and their ladies, all of whom found the French officers particularly charming.

Virginians began to celebrate Washington's birthday as early as 1779. Even though the commander-in-chief had not yet achieved a significant victory, they were already calling him the savior of his country and, with pardonable exaggeration, the brave asserter of the rights and liberties of all mankind. In Williamsburg the anniversary was observed with a discharge of thirteen salvos and the usual "elegant" entertainment—1780 it was a ball—at the town's social center, Raleigh Tavern. Fredericksburg, where the "illustrious chief" had family ties—he had spent some of his boyhood years here, and here was the home of his mother and his sister, Betty, Mrs. Fielding Lewis—celebrated with equal enthusiasm. The presence of two regiments of the Virginia Line on February 22, 1780, added much to the "rejoicings" of the day. At noon thirteen pieces of cannon discharged a "grand salute," succeeded by a *feu de joie* fired by the troops, who "cut a very martial appearance." In the evening there was a ball at the coffee house.

Virginians paid further homage to their most distinguished citizen by honoring his "amiable consort," "Lady Washington." When her "Ladyship" arrived in Williamsburg in August 1777 amidst the ringing of bells, she was saluted with volleys of artillery and small arms and conducted to Mrs. Elizabeth Dawson's house, where Washington had often dined when he was a member of the House of Burgesses. How to honor the plump little lady was decided at a meeting of the Common Hall. Here it was unanimously resolved that she should be presented the "most respectful testimony" of the high esteem in which "the illustrious defender and deliverer of his country" was held, that a golden emblematical medal should be struck and presented to the General's lady, and that she should convey the freedom of the city to "her illustrious consort." All this more than four years before Yorktown! What extraordinary confidence in a future that looked precarious!

Although the Association did not interdict dancing, it did "discountenance and discourage . . . expensive diversions and entertainments." Chief among these were balls, private and public, which required musicians, beverages, and food. Dancers there were always aplenty—young, old, married, single, white, and black (these last two not together, however). Virginians, exclaimed Fithian, would "dance or die!" That is, all Virginians except the noisily devout "Anabaptists," who would have liked to do away with all amusements, and ailing, irascible old men like Colonel Landon Carter, who thought that young people wasted too much time dancing. No well-conducted orchestras were needed to set the Virginians in rhythmic motion: on the frontier a fiddle would do; among the blacks, a banjo with four strings made from a gourd in imitation of a guitar; in the candle-lit ballrooms of the gentry several instruments, among them violin, French horn, and flute.

Virginians never missed an occasion to dance. If young men and women came together to dress flax, they ended up dancing. A boat race on the river called for a shipboard dance for both rowers and spectators. New Year's day produced dancing. Whenever a family moved into a house or repaired the one they had been living in, a ball and supper were in order. Christmas might be the occasion for ball; and so would a christening. Williamsburg climaxed its Saratoga victory celebration with a ball and banquet at the Capitol. On the frontier, wedding festivities ended with an all-night dance which reduced all participants except the bride and groom (who had been snugged away in the loft) to exhaustion. Here the figures of the dancers were three and four reels, or square sets and jigs. In these exhibitions of endurance, the dancers, when they became tired, could "cut out," that is, signal someone to take their places without there being any interruption of the dance. The fiddler was thus kept continuously at work. And if anyone attempted to steal forty winks in some dark corner, he was paraded on the cabin floor to the tune of "Hang on till to-morrow morning."

Blacks often danced at night after a long day's work, stimulated not only by their own naturally exuberant spirits, but also by ardent spirits occasionally supplied by the mansion. On Sunday, the one day they could call their own, they sometimes held dances, with the music provided by the banjo, drum, rattle, or their own deep-throated chants. In their songs they subtly referred to the usage they received at the hands of their master or mistresses.

Only the great planters had the wealth or facilities to give large dancing parties which sometimes lasted several days. Here the ladies, dressed in rustling silks, and gentlemen in ruffled shirts and smart waistcoats and breeches came to dine, drink, and dance to the tune of several instruments. First came the minuet, followed successively by jigs, reels, and country dances, sometimes interspersed with marches. Those who did not wish to dance played cards, drank (perhaps a little too much), offered patriotic toasts, or sang "Liberty Songs" in which six or more persons would put their heads together to emit "unharmonious" sounds. As many as seventy or more people might come together on one of these lavish occasions.

Dancing instruction was usual if one wanted to cut a fine figure. Probably the most highly regarded dancing master in eastern Virginia was Francis Christian, who called periodically at the mansions where there were young people. Williamsburg must have been delighted in 1775 to learn that Sarah Hallam, the estranged wife of the dissolute manager-actor of the American Company, Lewis Hallam, proposed to open a dancing school for young ladies. (She needed support for herself and her son, for her husband had gone to the West Indies.) Her charge for instruction on Fridays and Saturdays was twenty shillings at entrance and four pounds a year; satisfaction was guaranteed to her clients. Her school flourished, of course. Four years later John Kadow, recently arrived from France—as so many dancing masters proclaimed they had—notified the public that he would open a school for teaching both the minuet "in the neatest and newest manner," fencing, and French.

With so many devotees, dancing never really stopped during the Revolution. Occasionally a person such as poor Bennett White was haled before a county committee for having held a subscription ball accompanied by gaming. In this case the culprit was absolved after pleading his "uneasiness for having done any thing that had caused the displeasure of the committee" and reminding them that this was a first offense. Certainly by early 1777 "balls, assemblies, mirth and jollity" prevailed in the Virginia capital to set the tone for the rest of the province. With the arrival of the sophisticated, worldly French allies, social life in Virginia went into high gear after the victory at Yorktown. After all, there were no linguistic barriers to dancing and some other pleasures. In December the French commander-in-chief, Comte de Rochambeau, found time to give a splendid dinner and ball that delighted the guests. The Virginia ladies, recorded Baron Ludwig von Closen, an aide-de-camp to General Rochambeau, were very fond of the minuet, which they danced better than did the ladies up north, but they did not perform the schottische as well as the latter. Everyone liked the French quadrilles and, in general, found "French manners to their taste." So the balls became "endless," for Virginia belles loved dancing "with as much passion" as the men did hunting, horse-racing, and cock-fighting.

Not without justification did British wags poke fun at the restrictive provision of the Association regarding funerals. Throughout the colonies affluent people were accustomed to paying their last respects to loved ones elaborately and expensively. Those who served at funerals received either scarf, ring, or gloves; relatives of the deceased went into mourning dress; and mourners consumed quantities of food and drink at the obsequies.

In rural Virginia, where people might come from a distance to watch and grieve over the dead, the bereaved family was almost obliged to provide for them, but the three gallons of wine and nearly twenty gallons of spirits drunk at the funeral of John McClanahan in 1774 appear somewhat excessive.

Prior to the adoption of the Association there had been isolated efforts to regulate obsequies. In the 1640's the Virginia General Assembly had ordered that no one should expend powder unnecessarily at weddings and burials. Some years later one Edmund Watts, disgusted with "the debauched" drinking that went on at funerals, much to the dishonor of God and His true religion, left instructions in his will that no strong spirits were to be provided at his death. If during the Revolution there were violations of the funeral restraints ordered by the First Continental Congress, none was reported. Nevertheless, in 1777 Ambrose Davenport, a Williamsburg merchant, offered for sale among a large assortment of goods, men's mourning buckles and mourning fans; and among the ribbons and gloves that he had in stock, surely some of them must have been black.

III.

VIRGINIANS enjoyed some advantage in respect to health because very few of them lived in towns and nearly all of them produced the wholesome food served at their tables. As a result, smallpox, the most dreaded disease of the period, was less prevalent in Virginia than in some other areas, and the colony was spared serious epidemics such as those that occurred in Philadelphia and Boston. But Virginians did not have total immunity from the scourge, for despite quarantine laws, ships brought it to Virginia, as did slaves and transients. Virginians also suffered from ague—a recurring malarial fever marked by cold, hot, and sweating fits—tuberculosis, dysentery, apoplexy, cancer, and all the less formidable ailments such as the common cold. Many women died in the agony of puerperal fever, sometimes attended by only a midwife. No attention was given to preventive medicine, and thorough check-ups were unheard of.

As eighteenth-century physicians went, Virginia had several of considerable professional distinction who had obtained their medical training chiefly at the University of Edinburgh or had served an apprenticeship under a reputable doctor. There were no specialists among them; rather, they were men of remarkable versatility. Dr. Thomas Walker, for instance, was an explorer, a land speculator, an authority on Indian affairs, a soldier, a merchant, and a surveyor; Dr. Theodorick Bland was a poet of sorts, a soldier, and a legislator. Most of them, like the gallant Hugh Mercer, who was mortally wounded at the Battle of Princeton in 1777, had apothecary shops which were stocked not only with medicines, but also with spices, tea, soap, candy, syringes, and a variety of other items mostly imported from England.

Sometimes these druggist-doctors prescribed remedies and treatment on the basis of a written or a verbal description of the symptoms, or on order of the patient, whose self-diagnosis was perhaps as accurate as that resulting from an eighteenth-century medical examination. Surgery was still primitive, since doctors had little or no training and experience in this branch of the art of healing other than in the amputation of limbs. In addition, the lack of antiseptics and anesthetics (rum was used in lieu of these) ruled out most serious operations. Obstetrical cases were commonly entrusted to midwives who, from frequent practice (one was said to have brought more than 3,000 children into the world), must have acquired a degree of skill comparable to that of a doctor. Male midwives were available, but for modesty's sake most women preferred to be attended by members of their own sex.

There were also amateur doctors in Virginia, men whose medical education came from reading the contents of the *Materia Medica* in their libraries and from prescribing for themselves and members of their families, as well as servants and slaves. Such a one was Landon Carter, frequently troubled in his later years by "costiveness" and colic, to both of which he gave meticulous attention. After perusing the most recent medical works published abroad he would painstakingly record cures, one of which prescribed leeches to arrest cancer.

Quacks of both sexes abounded. One imposter promised to cure "CANCERS, CANKERS, MORTIFICATIONS, FISTULAS, POLYPUSSES, RINGWORMS of all kinds, the GRAVEL, DROPSY, DRY GRIPES," and other diseases; this genius also practiced "in every branch of SURGERY, MIDWIFERY and PHYSICK." Such was the fame of Constant Woodson of Prince Edward County for curing cancers that in 1767 the Virginia Assembly voted her a reward of one hundred pounds. But the following year the husband of one of her patients, who had had breast cancer, warned the public to beware of the "false pretensions of an unskilled physician," adding that his wife had grown much worse as a result of the "improper medicines" prescribed by Mrs. Woodson.

Considering the paucity and lack of skill of eighteenth-century hospitals, it was probably just as well that in Virginia the ill, with few exceptions, were cared for at home. Here they were attended by members of the family, "emulous to do them kind offices," were visited by neighbors, were given the "little rarities which their sickly appetites" might crave, and were administered home remedies or standard medicines, such as calomel and Epsom salts, that had been used for generations. Before the Revolution, though, there were at least two private hospitals in Virginia, if such one could call the plain wooden buildings which provided minimal comforts and crude nursing care, chiefly for surgical cases.

Not so was the hospital for the mentally ill in Williamsburg, the first such institution in America, which opened in 1773, under the trusteeship of some of the most distinguished Virginians. The two-story brick structure had twenty-four rooms, which were heated by "stoves fixed in the Partition between two rooms, with the Mouth open to the Passage, by which means they make fires and the mad People cannot come at them." The patients' diet was wholesome—water gruel, mush and molasses or rice with bread and butter or milk. Four days a week the patients were served meat, broth, vegetables, and a quart of small beer. The hospital received both men and women, blacks as well as whites.

There was at least one pesthouse in colonial Virginia located in the seaport town of Norfolk where, notwithstanding quarantine regulations, incoming ships brought contagious diseases from time to time. It was to such a hospital that Dr. Archibald Campbell of Norfolk took his patients in 1768 after his house was burned in protest of his having used it as a place of inoculation, over the objections of neighbors, who feared the premature dismissal of the patients.

In Virginia, as in other provinces, those submitting to inoculation against smallpox were usually members of the upper class who had some knowledge of medical developments. The general practice was for small groups of men and women to undergo inoculation together at some isolated place. Here these "classes," usually composed of friends, received medical and nursing care until they recovered from the disease. Since some of the patients were young people and unattached, it was rumored that romances occasionally developed during their period of confinement.

The public, though, was apprehensive of this newfangled technique for combating the incidence of the dread disease and petitioned the House of Burgesses to control inoculation. The response was the regulatory act of 1769. It stated that since the "wanton introduction" of smallpox by inoculation had proved a nuisance "by disturbing the peace and quietness" of many people and "exposing their lives to the infection of that mortal distemper" any person introducing "the small-pox, or any variolous or infectious matter of the said distemper" would be fined £1000. But the lawmakers admitted that inoculation "under peculiar circumstances" might very well be a "necessary means of securing those who are unavoidably exposed to the danger of taking the distemper in the natural way." For this reason, the act provided that if anyone thought himself exposed to an "immediate danger" of catching smallpox, he was to notify the chief magistrate of the county or town, who was then required to summon all the magistrates to consider whether in this particular case it might be "prudent or necessary or dangerous to the health and safety of the neighbourhood," to grant a license for inoculation. Anyone inoculating without a license would be fined £100 for each offense.

These stringent regulations undoubtedly discouraged, but did not eliminate, inoculation in colonial Virginia. For instance, when smallpox broke out in Winchester in 1771, several men were granted permission to inoculate. In 1772, Benjamin Harrison announced that since he was unable to check the progress of smallpox in his family, he would resort to inoculation and warned anyone who was not immune to avoid landing at Berkeley. As the law could not prevent a person from going out of the colony to be inoculated, some Virginians went to Maryland for that purpose. Baltimore doctors advertised for "customers" in the Virginia press and did a thriving business as a result.

Among those who went to Maryland for inoculation was George Washington's stepson, John Parke Custis, familiarly known as Jack. The young man left Mount Vernon in 1771 "with so many doubts and difficulties" about the matter that the family concluded that "nothing was more foreign from his Intention." This set the fears of his mother at rest. When Washington heard that Jack had indeed been inoculated, he withheld the news from his wife until the son's "perfect recovery." Washington's consideration fulfilled an oft-expressed wish on her part "that Jack wou'd take and go through the disorder without her knowing it; that she might escape those Tortures which Suspence w'd throw her into . . . ."

The care of the destitute devolved on the local vestry, who paid physicians to board and treat the ill; when the poor died, the vestry took care also of burial expenses. Funds for these purposes were obtained through assessments on the titheable persons of the parish. The indigent who had "no strength to labour" were also boarded in the houses of farmers. Seldom, if ever, did one meet a beggar, not only in Virginia, but also in the other provinces—a fact which

European visitors rarely failed to note. Masters were obligated to care for their sick or disabled servants, and if they circumvented this responsibility by a grant of freedom, they were charged ten pounds, payable to the churchwardens, and were also liable for damages.

Although the War for Independence in Virginia was responsible for thousands of casualties and for the increased spread of smallpox, it was not without good effects. For one thing, it brought to the state some well-trained and experienced foreign doctors, at least two of whom, Francis Joseph Mettauer of Alsace and Robert Wellford of Hertfordshire, England, remained. The proliferation of military hospitals during these violent years resulted in greater understanding of institutional care of the sick and wounded. The first important military hospital was located outside of Williamsburg on the road to York, and was variously known as the Vineyard, Continental, or Virginia Hospital.

Early in the Revolution the Governor's Palace was marked for conversion into a military hospital for Americans, but this change did not take place until the fall of 1781, when the little college town teemed with war casualties. The beautiful structure, so well adapted to entertainment but so ill-suited for a hospital, burned to the ground in December of that year. Fortunately, all of the patients were saved. The sick and wounded among the French were treated in the main building and the President's House of the College of William and Mary, to the chagrin and certainly the discomfort of the members of that institution. On November 23, 1781, the President's House was gutted by fire, but not before the patients had been carried to safety. Other military hospitals were located at York, Hampton, Portsmouth, Fredericksburg, Alexandria, Chesterfield Court House, and probably at other places. The hospital at Gloucester, in operation as late as March 1782, was used to care for British sick and wounded.

The most significant medical progress in Virginia during the war was the change in the public attitude toward inoculation; of considerable consequence was the example set by Virginia's own General George Washington. The commander-in-chief not only ordered his troops and his servants to be inoculated, but also persuaded the members of his family to do likewise. His wife was at first hesitant. In the spring of 1776 he said that Mrs. Washington was talking about "taking the Small Pox," but that he doubted "her resolution." The following year, however, the General could report that "my whole Family, I understand, are likely to get well through the disorder with no other assistance than that of Doctor Lund." In discussing the matter, he discounted the pretensions of the medical "faculty" to exclusive competence in performing inoculation. In general, he explained, "an old Woman may Inoculate with as much success as the best Physician, the whole Art lying in keeping the Patient rather low in diet, and cool, especially at the period of the eruptive fever . . . ." Surely, he believed, the time had come to repeal the "Impolitic Act, restraining Inoculation in Virginia" and substitute a law "to compel the Masters of Families to inoculate every Child born within a certain limited time under severe Penalties."

The legislative response did not go so far as Washington recommended, but the act of 1777 to amend the act of 1769 did reflect a more progressive attitude toward inoculation. Whereas the earlier measure had stated that inoculation was an unnecessary nuisance, the second one recognized that "the late discoveries and improvements" had produced "great benefits to mankind" by rendering the distemper comparatively mild and safe through inoculation. The provisions, though, were still cumbersome. First of all, anyone wishing to inoculate or to be inoculated had to obtain the consent of a majority of the housekeepers residing with two miles; during the period of quarantine the patient's movements were carefully regulated; anyone undertaking inoculation had to notify the public in writing that the smallpox was at such and such a house; if inoculation was administered at a public place or hospital, the doctor was not to discharge a patient before he was "sufficiently cleansed"; and anyone who had not had smallpox and yet visited a patient was to be sent to a smallpox hospital and confined there until he had "gone through the distemper" or given proof of immunity. Violations of these regulations were subject to fines. Now, at least, one could obtain inoculation without having previously been exposed to the disease.

Both civilians and soldiers suffered from the scarcity of medicines during the Revolution. Even such standard remedies as calomel, tartar emetic, camphor, myrrh, Peruvian bark, Virginia snakeroot, and jalap were high in price and not always obtainable. Many Virginians, however, probably took this situation in the same spirit displayed by Richard Henry Lee in 1778: "For the greatest part of my life I have been used to Wine and Jesuits Bark [cinchona] & now I have neither—It goes hard with me—But the establishment of public liberty smooths all ways however rugged." Fortunately, his doctor-diplomat brother, Arthur Lee, was eventually able to supply him with the bark on which Virginians relied to ward off malaria.

The doctors had no easy time of it during the war years, which brought spiraling inflation along with difficulties in obtaining the tools of their trade. As early as 1776 Doctors William Pasteur and John Minson Galt of Williamsburg requested their customers to settle medical accounts, at least those of a year's standing; this request, they said, was not unreasonable since they had to pay for medicines with cash. During the inflationary crisis Virginia was fortunate in having an acceptable medium of exchange, tobacco, in use since the infancy of the Old Dominion. In 1779, for instance, one doctor announced that his fees remained unchanged: a day's visit, five shillings; an emetic, two shillings, sixpence "either in commodities that he needs or in Tobacco at twenty shillings per hundred weight, or money [specie]." In a similar advertisement, Dr. James Currie stated that his fees would be at the old rate, but payable in tobacco at the value quoted above.

In 1780 four "Practitioners of Physick and Surgery" in Fredericksburg gave notice that since they had been disadvantaged for the past two years by the fluctuating state of the currency, the high price of medicines, and the impossibility of getting accounts fairly settled, they would extend their services at the 1774 rates and receive payment in produce at old prices or in money equivalent to the selling price of commodities at the time of payment. A group of five Petersburg doctors published a like statement, claiming that in the future they would do business only with those who could supply them with "corn, wheat, pork, Virginia cloth, or any other article needed by ourselves or families." Dr. Edmund Wilcox, who practiced in Buckingham and Amherst counties, usually charged 40 pounds of tobacco per visit in 1777, 40 and occasionally 50 pounds in 1778, and these rates continued through some of the war years except in special cases. For instance, the charge for a day's attendance might run as high as 200 pounds. The fee for thirty-six hours of attendance on "Negro Sue" in 1781 was 400 pounds of tobacco. Once the busy doctor received a mare in lieu of 4,000 pounds of tobacco for medicines; and another time 30 yards of linen for use as shirting for slaves. Rarely was payment accepted in current money, and then only at inflationary rates.

Dr. David Ramsay, the first major historian of the American

Revolution, wrote shortly after the end of hostilities that "surgery was one of the arts which was promoted by the war." Prior to the conflict, he explained "from the want of hospitals and other aids, the medical men of America had few opportunities of perfecting themselves in this art, the thorough knowledge of which can only be acquired by practice and observation. The melancholy events of battles gave the American students an opportunity of seeing and learning more in one day than they could have acquired in years of peace." Especially were such opportunities available in Virginia, where local doctors watched skilled French surgeons at work and heard them discourse learnedly on medicine. A further broadening of medical education came as a result of travel with the army and association with other American doctors. Although there were no medical journals until after the Revolution, increased personal and epistolary contact between doctors disseminated the latest medical breakthroughs, such as the important cure for lockjaw discovered by the Revolution's most eminent physician, Benjamin Rush. And the clinical emphasis of American practice probably furthered medical science as much as did the artificial experiments and theoretical controversies which absorbed their European counterparts.

IV.

"ART and education have not yet attained the degree of perfection found in Europe," observed Baron von Closen while he was in Virginia during the Revolution. Yet thoughtful Virginians had been concerned about the education of their children ever since the infancy of the Old Dominion. The "free" schools that had been founded in the colony through private philanthropy, such as the Syms and Eaton schools in Hampton, were free only to children of the poor, but other children were doubtless admitted at little or no cost.

Robert Beverley in describing the Virginia scene at the opening of the eighteenth century stated that there were "large tracts of land, houses and other things granted to free schools," some of them so large that they were "a handsome maintenance to a master." These schools, he said, had been established by "the legacies of well-inclined gentlemen" and the supervision of them was left to the county courts or the vestry. The benefactor of such a facility sometimes referred to it as "my school" and controlled the teacher whose salary he paid. Yet Landon Carter did not dismiss the master of his charity school, "a pert Prigg" in Carter's opinion, because the people whose children he taught liked him. Even on the frontier, education was not totally neglected; one of the victims of Indian warfare in the Greenbrier Valley in 1755 was an anonymous schoolmaster, who probably exchanged with the pioneers a mite of instruction for board.

Some planters preferred to hire tutors and governesses to educate their children despite the expense of maintaining the instructors in genteel fashion and occasionally paying for their passage from Britain. Although a tutor like John Harrower on the plantation of Colonel William Daingerfield was legally only an indentured servant, he was well treated (except when Mrs. Daingerfield objected to his

33

disciplinary methods) and enjoyed the added advantage of being able to earn a few extra pounds by teaching the children of neighbors. Philip Fithian was a respected member of the household of Robert Carter, and for his services in teaching English to the five daughters and Latin, Greek, and English to the three sons he received a yearly stipend of £60 plus accommodations, including his board, a private room, a horse and servant, and access to one of the finest libraries in Virginia. And there were other "considerable" openings for educators in Virginia. In 1772 Landon Carter paid £30 to George Menzie, the tutor of his grandchildren, during a period of probation, or, as the testy master of Sabine Hall put it, "until he convinced me that he was a proper person for such a Concern." It turned out that he was not; for one thing, he permitted the schoolroom to become greasy and dirty and "wet with Piss and Nastyness."

Mrs. George Turberville of Westmoreland County engaged an English governess, Miss Sally Panton, to teach French and English to her daughter Letty. The young governess, reported Fithian, owned an estate in England that produced £50 sterling annually and wore attire that elicited some spiteful comments from the social circle in which she moved in Virginia. In 1778 the still unmarried governess, who had by then been hired by Richard Henry Lee, decided to return home. This decision troubled her new employer because he had only paper money with which to pay her, and such currency was not acceptable abroad.

The apex of the educational structure of colonial Virginia was the College of William and Mary, established in 1693 for the purpose of educating the white youth of Virginia, training ministers for the Anglican Church, and converting heathen Indians. By 1770 the president of the College received £200 annually; two professors of divinity, one of moral philosophy, and one of natural philosophy each earned £100; and a professor of humanity or master of the grammar school received £150. All of them were clergymen.

The College personnel included ushers (assistant teachers), masters of the Indian school, a bursar (treasurer), a gardener, a housekeeper, clerks, a librarian, a janitor, a surveyor of the woodcutters, and a writing master. The professors augmented their income by taking each his turn as college chaplain and filling nearby pulpits; and the president enjoyed the use of not only a house and garden, but also pay for serving on the Governor's Council. On the basis of faculty qualifications, salaries, and alumni achievement, William and Mary

The Main Building of the College of William and Mary. Now known as the Wren Building. *Courtesy of Colonial Williamsburg Foundation.*

ranked high among colonial colleges, but Richard Henry Lee, who was partial to an English education, felt that not enough attention was paid there "either to the learning, or morals" of the students.

In order to afford his sons a "well grounded knowledge of eloquence, Civil, and natural law" in preparation for the study of law and subsequent government service, Lee solicited his brothers, William and Arthur, then living abroad, for help in placing the Lee boys in proper schools. Richard Henry Lee had himself been sent to England at the age of twelve to study at an academy in Wakefield run by the Reverend Benjamin Wilson, while his older brothers, Philip Ludwell Lee and Thomas Ludwell Lee, were at the Inner Temple studying law. His younger brother Arthur Lee had gone to Eton and then to the University of Edinburgh, where he had graduated in medicine. After coming home his decision to go into public service had sent him back to England to study law at Lincoln's Inn and the Middle Temple.

The Lees, all of whom had had the advantage of tutors at home in Westmoreland County, were not unique in preferring to complete their education abroad. Ignoring the danger of smallpox infection, Virginians sent their children to English grammar schools, and to Dalston, Harrow, Appleby, Winchester, Leeds, and Eton, as well as to Cambridge, Oxford, Edinburgh, Aberdeen, and the Inns of Court.

The Revolution did not slacken the normal thirst for learning in Virginia or impede to any discernible extent educational progress except during the climactic interval when the state became the main theatre of war. As before, education continued to be a private responsibility. The hiring of teachers was left to parents, benefactors, and trustees, but their task was eventually rendered difficult because the immigration of English instructors stopped during the conflict. One of the last schoolmasters to come to Virginia arrived on the *Justitia* in March 1775, along with more than a hundred "healthy servants," most of whom were skilled laborers.

The number of "help wanted" advertisements—more numerous than those of "situations wanted"—some of which ran for several issues despite the rising cost of inserting them, indicates that the pedagogical job market was favorable to teachers during the Revolutionary years. Tutors capable of teaching ancient and modern languages and mathematics were most in demand; besides "genteel" salaries they were offered such fringe benefits as washing, lodging, mending, and a horse. Recommendations were often required. In 1777 Mann Page offered £60 for a well-recommended tutor, who was assured that he would be treated in every respect like one of the family.

The pay was the same as that proposed by some subscribers in Warwick and York counties for a single woman able to teach twelve or fifteen children—most of them girls—in reading, writing, and needlework. But such stipends became unrealistic as inflation rose in Virginia and the rest of the country. In advertising for "a Gentleman of character and liberal education" to teach three boys, Theodorick Bland of Prince George County in 1780 offered a salary fixed in the "commodities of the country," in order to secure the applicant against the "ill effects" of the decline in the purchasing power of the currency. In lieu of a fixed salary, "very great encouragement," was also proffered to teachers.

Some of those seeking situations as teachers were women who claimed to be well-qualified to instruct young ladies in the three R's, needlework including the popular tambour, and occasionally guitar playing and French. Day students were preferred, but Mrs. Neill of Williamsburg offered also to find board, lodgings, and other accommodations for any girls who might wish to enroll in her school; and as an additional inducement she promised to provide dancing instruction from the "best masters." One lady who not only was professedly skilled in "household economy," "mantua-making," and needlework, but was also prepared to teach the three R's, offered her services to a "genteel family" as governess for young ladies, or as a companion or an assistant. Obviously she desperately needed a place.

As before the Revolution, schools already or about to be established advertised their services. The Littleton School in Cumberland County, for instance, which in September 1775 had one master, promised that by the following month it would be attended by two masters of good education, who would teach Greek, Latin, and mathematics in all its branches, and by a third master who would teach natural and moral philosophy. Planters in the neighborhood of the school could accommodate 40 boys at an annual rate per student of £10 for bed, board, and washing, and £5 for tuition. The promoters of this educational enterprise piously hoped that when peace was restored, a sufficient sum could be raised to support Littleton School "*in perpetuum*." The need for attention to morals in keeping with the doctrines of the Church of England was felt by the

Reverend Mr. Anderson and Mr. Swinton in Sussex, who proposed to open a school at the glebe for instruction in Latin and Greek as well as the mechanical arts, English literature, writing, accounts, geography, and mathematics.

Board could be had in the neighborhood for £12 though without bedding; tuition was £5 a year. This was what Adam Goadley charged pupils of Culpeper Grammar School; with bedding the rate was £15. At the height of inflation, school heads either raised the rates or asked that payments be made in commodities. For instance in January 1780 the Trustees of Washington Henry Academy in Hanover County gave notice that tuition would be £120 and board £500, one half of the money to be paid at entrance and the other half in six months.

From the standpoint of curriculum, no school was a match for one in King and Queen County, scheduled to open in January 1778 under the direction of Daniel Mara, A. M. Here, it was said, youth could receive instruction in Arabic, Greek, Latin, French, Italian, rhetoric, logic, ancient and modern history, geography, writing, arithmetic, bookkeeping, and some branches of mathematics. Not even the College of William and Mary could offer such varied fare. Doubtless the extension of horizons during the Revolution emphasized an urgency for the study of modern languages.

The Virginians' recognition that the "education and morals of youth" were imperative objectives led to the founding of two schools that today are part of Virginia's galaxy of higher institutions. The first of these, present Washington and Lee University, began in 1749 as Augusta Academy on a site twenty miles north of Lexington. This upland institution, a product of the Scotch-Irish infiltration of the Valley of Virginia, was the first school west of the Blue Ridge. In 1776 the school was moved to Timber Ridge in Augusta County, an "exceeding pleasant, healthy, and plentiful" locality, and was appropriately renamed Liberty Hall Academy. The curriculum consisted of the "most important branches of literature necessary to prepare young gentlemen for the study of law, physick, and theology."

Already the school had a "considerable library of well chosen books, and the most essential parts of a mathematical and philosophical apparatus." Tuition was fixed at £4 per annum, and board at £6-10s, one third of the latter to be paid at entrance; wood was provided gratis, but the students were responsible for their beds, washing, and candles. The act of incorporation passed in 1782 made

Liberty Hall Academy a degree-granting institution and required its professors, masters, and tutors to take an oath of fidelity to the commonwealth; they, as well as students under twenty-one, were exempt from military service.

Hampden-Sydney Academy in Prince Edward County also opened in 1776 under the presidency of Samuel Stanhope Smith, a Presbyterian divine and former professor at the College of New Jersey, who had married the daughter of its president, John Witherspoon, a signer of the Declaration of Independence. In 1779 Smith returned to Princeton and was replaced by his brother John Blair Smith, who had graduated with honors from that institution in 1773. The course of study adopted by the trustees and the president of the Prince Edward County school was, not surprisingly, similar to that of the College of New Jersey save that a "more particular attention" was to be paid to the cultivation of the English language.

Here, too, the students had the benefit of a library and the apparatus to facilitate the study of mathematics and natural philosophy. The steward, an increasingly difficult position to fill as inflation advanced, was responsible for providing a "good and wholesome" diet to students at the initial rate of £8 annually, one-fourth to be paid at entrance. The students had to see to their beds, candles, and washing, but they could obtain wood from the land belonging to the academy.

The Presbyterian character of the school, discernible in the choice of staff, drew some sectarian fire, despite assurances that some of the visitors were members of the Anglican Church and that parents could require their children to attend any religious service they pleased. "Luther," an anonymous spokesman for intolerance, charged that it was highly imprudent to suffer a dissenter, a Presbyterian, to teach in any school, much less to act as president, for such a person, unexceptionable though his character might be, could not fail to impose the "detestable doctrines" of predestination, reprobation, and the "final perseverance of Saints" on the theologically naive students, particularly if they were exposed to the study of divinity. The inevitable consequences of employing dissenting masters would be the appearance of dissenters in gowns and cassocks, a sight that should be avoided at all cost.

Samuel Stanhope Smith's reply to this man of "narrow principles" was judiciously restrained: his own conduct and the reputation of his scholars would provide his vindication. The act for incorporating

Hampden-Sydney Academy, passed in 1783, enabled the school to grant degrees; it also required that the teachers, through their counduct, manifest to the world their "sincere affection for the liberty and independence of the United States." This was in conformity with the final statement of the College charter of June 28, 1783: "the greatest care and caution shall be used in electing such professors and masters, to the end that no person shall be so elected unless the uniform tenor of his conduct manifests to the world his sincere affection for the liberty and independence of the United States."

In contrast to this education progress in the hinterland of Virginia, the College of William and Mary experienced some dark days during the Revolution as a result of military operations and inflation, both of which sharply reduced enrollments. In addition, Williamsburg in 1780 was divested of its political importance by the removal of the capital of Virginia to Richmond.

Inflation, which peaked in 1780, imposed drastic adjustments on the part of both professors and students of the College of William and Mary. President James Madison wrote President Ezra Stiles of Yale that during the Revolution the former resources of the College had been "almost annihilated." "From a Revenue of 5 or 6000£ Stg. a year ᵂᶜ· arose principally from Duties on Articles of Commerce," he explained, "it now depends for its support upon ye Rent of 22000 acres of Land, ᵂᶜ· in Time will become considerable, but at present does not afford more than 500£ sterlg.—There is indeed also an Income from Surveys, but not very considerable."

Before 1779, William and Mary accepted rents in current money instead of in tobacco or sterling. After that date it began to issue stern warnings to the college tenants to pay their rents in tobacco or money at the current price of tobacco. Later, only tobacco was declared acceptable. In December 1779 the Board of Visitors of William and Mary ordered that each professor should receive 1,000 pounds of tobacco annually for every student who attended his classes. Student fees were also assessed in tobacco—1,000 pounds for two classes and 1,500 for three, to be paid at entrance. The college dining room was abolished, and students had to find board wherever they could after someone who had agreed to furnish breakfast and dinner to as many as twenty students at 3,000 pounds of tobacco each year had a change of mind because of the exorbitant cost of necessaries.

The students complained at what they regarded as unreasonable exactions. Some withdrew, others remained, but they were obliged to enroll in fewer courses because professorial fees made too heavy demands on their lean purses. Undergraduate John Brown reported pessimistically that "Board & entring under two Professors amounts to 4,000 wt. of Tobacco." He feared, therefore, that he would be unable to attend Professor Wythe's lectures. Already he had had to drop French, in which he had made progress, "for no other reason than that the Visitors raised the price of attendance on that Branch to a Hd of Tobacco." As if academic frustrations were not enough, in the fall of 1780 an enemy invasion put to flight Mr. Cocke, with whom Brown had been boarding. Only a stout heart and a passion for learning could induce one to remain in college under such conditions. "The Town [is] almost deserted," wrote Brown, now become ill and dejected, "no Meat so that I run the risk of suffering for provisions. I am so weak that I cannot leave my Room in the College which is intirely deserted by every Studt but one or two who are sick . . . ."

Yet, notwithstanding these troubles, the College of William and Mary emerged from the struggle for independence institutionally strengthened and more attuned than before to the needs and spirit of the times. And it was a small group of students from the College who met almost five months after the adoption of the Declaration of Independence to organize the Phi Beta Kappa Society, the first and now the most prestigious intercollegiate honorary society. From the outset the roster of this society included names that were to become notable, and their number increased as chapters were established in other institutions beginning with Harvard and Yale in 1779.

Early in the conflict (1777) President John Camm, a graduate of Cambridge University and a staunch champion of the rights and privileges of the Anglican Church, was dismissed because of his loyalist principles. His successor was the Reverend James Madison, a second cousin of President James Madison and a 1772 graduate of the College of William and Mary, which had awarded him the Botetourt medal for distinction in the classics. In 1775 he went to England for ordination and remained there until the following year to continue secular studies.

Madison, an ardent whig, was only twenty-eight years old at the time of his appointment to the College presidency; therefore the law requiring the incumbent to be no younger than thirty had to be suspended. The other members of the small faculty were also well trained: George Wythe, the professor of law, had been a student at

William and Mary and had earned a reputation for his penetrating lectures on municipal and constitutional law; James McClurg, the professor of medicine, was also an alumnus of the College as well as of the University of Edinburgh, where he had studied medicine; Robert Andrews, the professor of moral philosophy, was a graduate of the College of Philadelphia (later the University of Pennsylvania); and Charles Bellini, a capable linguist, was the professor of modern languages. By any standard, this was a superior faculty.

Still, the College needed curricular, administrative, and fiscal improvement, and no one recognized this more than Thomas Jefferson, whose "Bill for Amending the Constitution of the College of William and Mary, and Substituting More Certain Revenues for Its Support" reflects the author's catholicity, imaginativeness, and attention to detail. The bill did not pass. But when Jefferson in 1779 became both Governor of Virginia and a Visitor of the College, he succeeded in abolishing the grammar school, which he thought "filled the college with children" cutting their educational teeth on Latin and Greek and rendered "it disagreeable and degrading to young gentlemen already prepared for entering on the sciences."

Jefferson wanted nothing less than to transform William and Mary into a university. The visitors abolished also the two professorships for divinity and further moved toward total secularization by instituting professorships for: (1) Law and Police; (2) Anatomy and Medicine; (3) Natural Philosophy and Mathematics; (4) Moral Philosophy, the Law of Nature and Nations, and the Fine Arts; and (5) Modern Languages.

The Brafferton fund professorships, which had been established through the philanthropy of the English scientist Robert Boyle for the purpose of Christianizing the Indians, were retained; but Jefferson hoped that in time the funds would be converted to "maintaining a perpetual mission among the Indian tribes, the object of which, besides instructing them in the principles of Christianity, . . should be to collect their traditions, laws, customs, languages, and other circumstances which might lead to a discovery of their relation with one another, or descent from other nations." And such investigation would be extended from tribe to tribe.

If Jefferson's proposal had been followed, the College of William and Mary would have had the distinction of establishing the first department of anthropology in America. Jefferson hoped also to add a chair for "antient languages and literature of the North"—Anglo-

Saxon, as it is presently labeled—which he thought merited study because of its relationship with the language, laws, customs, and history of England. But this also was impossible at the time.

The education of Virginians did not end with the termination of their formal training, for they were avid readers and often turned to books for guidance and pleasure. Probably all literate Virginians had at least a Bible and a few other works of a religious tone, such as John Bunyan's *Pilgrim's Progress*, the *Book of Common Prayer*, and Isaac Watts' *Hymns,* in addition to the indispensable spelling and grammar books. In contrast to these meager holdings were the rich private libraries of Virginia's men of culture, notably those of William Byrd II, Robert Carter of Nomini Hall, and Thomas Jefferson, all discriminating bibliophiles, who sometimes strained their eyes by "too great desire for knowledge."

The largest of the libraries was that of William Byrd II of Westover, which, along with "philosophical instruments" and engravings, was put up for sale in 1777 after the death of the owner. The nearly four thousand works in the collection were shelved in twenty-three double presses of black walnut and were arranged under the classifications of History and Travel; Law; "Physick"; "Entertainment, Poetry, Translations &c."; Divinity; "French Books Chiefly of Entertainment"; Classics; and Unclassified.

The most impressive section of the library consisted of historical works and travel literature, which covered every period and part of the world; some of the books must have been illustrated. Books of poetry were numerous, but fiction was limited to such best sellers as *Don Quixote, Gargantua, Pantagruel, Gil Blas,* and *Tom Jones.* The texts were in modern and ancient languages. There was, of course, a large sprinkling of self-help works on medicine, law, and husbandry—all doubtless frequently consulted.

Although the library at Nomini Hall was smaller than the one at Westover, it was perhaps more versatile and reflective of the owner's taste. For one thing, it contained a number of musical compositions, particularly those of Handel. These were probably much used, since in the Carter household one heard the harpsichord, harmonica, forte-piano, guitar, violin, German flute, and organ. And the charming Mrs. Carter must have enjoyed the sentimental novels in the family library.

Such books were acquired over a long period, either on order from abroad or at Williamsburg. The leading bookseller in the Virginia capital was the firm of Dixon and Hunter, printers of the *Virginia Gazette*. At the start of the War for Independence it had well over 250 titles to offer to the public—approximately 71 of them religious works; 31 practical; 27 medical; 24 historical; 10 travel. There were, of course, dictionaries—18 of them. It also had a good assortment of fiction: *Humphrey Clinker, Peregrine Pickle, Pamela, Robinson Crusoe, Roderick Random, Tristram Shandy, The Vicar of Wakefield,* and the ever-popular *Tom Jones.*

Within a year the list of books had been greatly reduced; gone were nearly all of the novels, which in neighboring North Carolina were the hardest to sell. By 1779 the number of titles advertised in the *Gazette* had shrunk still more, an obvious result of the cessation of trade with Great Britain, from which country most of the books came. But Virginians could still purchase the *Virginia Almanack* as well as domestic periodicals and newspapers, and these contained some of the practical information they were ever needing and seeking.

The leadership provided by Virginia during the early years of the Republic was not a matter of accident. It was, rather, the product of a cultivated, responsible society whose elite had the resources and leisure to develop their intellectual potential. Their understanding of the subtleties of politics was penetrating. They enjoyed poetry, too, not only the great masterpieces of the ancient world and of the Tudor period, but also those of Milton, Dryden, and Pope. Absorbers they were in full measure; but creators, only to a very limited extent. Even in their favorite field of political philosophy, they produced little that was original, as Jefferson and Madison would have been the first to admit. Because they were practical men, destiny cast them as leaders, not as heroes. But perhaps that was the role that they preferred.

The educational achievements in Virginia during the Revolutionary War were, however, exclusive in origin and scope; schooling continued to be a privilege rather than a right for everyone. Remarkable as was the state's leadership at this time, it withheld support of Jefferson's "Bill for the More General Diffusion of Knowledge," which envisioned a system of public education that would have given preeminence to Virginia and would have expanded her ruling elite beyond the circle of her first families.

V.

ALTHOUGH religion was not a major motive in founding Virginia, the settlers who came to Jamestown in 1607 saw to the planting of the Church of England immediately on their arrival in the vast new world. The first minister was the stout-hearted Robert Hunt, and the first house of worship a wattle and daub building.

In time, as the brooding ruin of the brick church at Jamestown attests, such structures became larger and were more solidly constructed. Pious members of the burgeoning parishes donated altar pieces, fonts, Bibles, silver communion plate, silk and velvet pulpit hangings, and carpets; and the pews of the important parishioners became more impressive.

On their death some communicants were laid in inscribed stone tombs that still attract the visitors to Virginia churchyards. Sunday observance and church attendance were required by law, and those who failed to comply were fined. But as the eighteenth century progressed, people began to do what they pleased on Sunday— sporting, fishing, and drinking—and they got away with such conduct. Although the gentry ostentatiously continued to attend church, they apparently went less for their souls' sake than for the pleasure of seeing friends and neighbors and discussing temporal matters. Philip Vickers Fithian, a Presbyterian, slyly observed that at the Virginia churches there were three "grand divisions" of time on Sundays: " . . . before Service giving & receiving letters of business, reading Advertisements, consulting about the price of Tobacco, Grain &c. & settling either lineage, Age, or qualities of favorite Horses 2. In the Church at Service, prayrs read over in haste, a Sermon seldom under and never over twenty minutes, but always made up of sound morality, or deep studied Metaphysicks. 3. After

Service . . . three quarters of an hour spent in strolling round the Church among the Crowd," during which time dinner invitations were extended and accepted.

The decline in piety among Anglicans was in sharp contrast to the rise in zeal among the dissenters, who came to Virginia in large number during the several decades before the Revolution. The most substantial of these groups were the Presbyterians, many of whom migrated from Northern Ireland and settled in the Shenandoah Valley. Some were men of education—many of their ministers were graduates of the College of New Jersey—who possessed books and provided schooling for their children; even the women were not devoid of learning, and they, like the men, kept abreast of contemporary events.

Baptist ministers preached with the intensity of ancient prophets, and for their zeal, they suffered persecution. The first instance of imprisonment occurred in Spotsylvania County on June 4, 1768, when the sheriff seized several ministers, including John Waller of Spotsylvania County. At their trial one of the lawyers for the prosecution informed the court that these men were "great disturbers of the peace," unable to "meet a man upon the road" without trying to "ram a text of scripture down his throat." But certain as they were of eventually exchanging cross for crown, there was no restraining these men of God: they sang as they went to prison, preached from behind bars, and patiently bore all manner of insults, one of which was for some tormentor "to ride into the water, and make sport" while the minister was performing baptism. For their uncompromising position that a true Christian should make profession of faith at the time of baptism, which meant that he must be old enough to have a sense of conscience, that is, an awareness that he was being called by God to His faith, the Baptists elicited unfavorable comments even from their evangelical brethren, the Methodists. Unlike their Anglican and Presbyterian counterparts, the Baptist preachers, admitted Robert B. Semple, "were without learning, without patronage, generally very poor, very plain in their dress, unrefined in their manners, and awkward in their address," but through their "enterprising zeal and unwearied perseverance" they overcame these disadvantages and steadily gained converts.

It has been said that "Colonial Virginia was the first important seed plot of American Methodism," indeed "the cradle of Methodism" in this country. When it is remembered that Methodism developed as an evangelical movement within the Anglican Church, the reasons for Virginia's role in the rise of Methodism are obvious: in Virginia the Church of England was firmly established, Anglican priests were available to administer to Methodists the sacraments of baptism and communion; and Anglican churches were generally open to Methodist groups.

Moreover, in tolerant, spiritually easy-going Virginia, where the personal conduct of ministers was not always the most exemplary and the service was rigidly formalized, a revival movement like the Methodist was bound to succeed. The Methodist cause in Virginia was also fortunate in receiving the cooperation of a remarkable native, the Reverend Devereux Jarratt of New Kent County, ordained a deacon by the Bishop of London in December 1762. While in England, Jarratt heard John Wesley and George Whitefield preach, and on his return to Virginia proclaimed the gospel as passionately as they did. For his preaching he incurred the hostility of some Anglican clergy. Through his efforts and those of Robert Williams and Joseph Pilmoor, Methodism gained an impetus that was to be sustained through the missionary efforts of Francis Asbury.

Asbury first came to Virginia from England on April 29, 1775. Landing at Norfolk, he preached to a group of about thirty persons congregated in a ramshackle building that had formerly been a playhouse. The Methodists, like the Baptists, displayed in the course of their meetings such emotionalism as to offend both laymen and clergy accustomed to a formal pattern of worship. Nicholas Cresswell labeled the Methodists a set of "Canting, Whining Hypocrites," "Fag-end-of-the-Scripture mongers," "the noisiest Fellows" he had ever heard, all of them given to substituting noise for logic. Yet the religious ardor and circuitriding of the Methodists brought the gospel to the westerners and to poor people who had come to regard the Anglican parish as the bailiwick of the privileged.

The Revolution had a tremendous impact on religion in Virginia. Even before the conflict, dissenters in the colony, particularly the vociferous Baptists, had been urging the disestablishment of the Church of England, freedom of worship, and liberalization of marriage laws. A Baptist petition of May 1774, for instance, complained that a legislative proposal which would confine public worship to the daytime "was inconsistent with the laws of England, as well as the practice and usage of the primitive Churches, and even of the English Church itself; . . . "

The religious malcontents of every denomination found irrefutable argument in the last provision of the Virginia Declaration of Rights, adopted on June 12, 1776, which stated:

> That religion, or the duty which we owe to our CREATOR, and the manner of discharging it, can be directed only by reason and conviction, not by force or violence, and therefore, all men are equally entitled to the free exercise of religion, according to the dictates of conscience. . . .

This Magna Charta of Virginia inspired dissenters, such as the Presbytery of Hanover, to petition the General Assembly to secure them the promised freedom. For certain it was, they contended, "that every argument for civil liberty" gained "additional strength when applied to liberty in the concerns of religion," there being no argument in favor of establishing the Christian religion but what might be pled for establishing "the tenets of Mahomed by those who believe the Alkoran . . . . "

The first response to this kind of memorial was the passage by the Virginia legislature in October 1776, of an act exempting nonconformists from contributing to the support and maintenance of the Established Church and suspending payment of salaries to the Anglican clergy. But it reserved to the church its tracts of glebe land, its churches and chapels, and its books, plate, and ornaments. This did not totally disestablish the Church of England, though it went a long way in that direction. Nor did it repeal all the laws interfering with religious freedom. Still at issue was whether the maintenance of churches should be left to voluntary contributors or whether everyone should be assessed for the support of the pastor of his choice.

Moreover, as Jefferson explained in his *Notes On the State of Virginia*, published in 1785, anyone brought up in the Christian religion who denied the being of a God, or the trinity, or asserted that there was more than one God, or denied that Christianity was the true religion or that the Scriptures were of divine authority, still suffered severe disabilities. "Religious slavery" Jefferson called this situation and he would have ended it in 1779 by means of his great bill for "Establishing Religious Freedome."

Its lengthy preamble provided philosophical justification for total religious toleration, for separation of state and church, and for intellectual liberty. The two provisions of the bill went straight to the point: (1) " . . . no man shall be compelled to frequent or support any religious worship, place, or ministry whatsoever nor shall be enforced, retrained, molested, or burthened in his body or goods, nor shall otherwise suffer, on account of his religious opinions or beliefs . . . . " (2) " . . . the rights hereby asserted are of the natural rights of mankind, and that if any act shall be hereafter passed to repeal the present or to narrow its operation, such act will be an infringement of natural rights." This memorable counterpart to the Declaration of Independence, of which Jefferson was justly proud, was finally passed early in 1786.

The liberalization of the marriage laws was doubtless the result of prodding from the dissenters and the recognition of the fact that in the isolated western pockets of the state it was virtually impossible to enforce the existing laws. In October 1780 an act was passed recognizing the validity of marriages celebrated by ministers other than those of the Church of England, or, in the case of the Quakers and Mennonites, performed according to the rules and usages of their societies.

For everyone except members of these last two sects, marriage licenses or the publication thrice of banns was required. Marriage fees for ministers were fixed at the equivalent in money of twenty-five pounds of tobacco; ten pounds was charged for registering a marriage. County courts were empowered to license no more than four ministers of each sect per county for the performance of matrimony. In May 1783 the legislature continued the liberalizing trend by passing an act "to authorize and confirm marriages in certain cases." The preamble stated that many people in the remote areas of the commonwealth were "destitute of any persons, authorized by law" to solemnize marriages.

To meet this situation, the courts in any counties where there was a shortage of ministers were empowered to nominate "sober and discreet laymen" to supply the deficiency; after taking the oath of allegiance to the state, they were licensed to celebrate marriage according to the forms and customs of the church of which they were members. Further regulation came with the act of October 1784, which required ministers to obtain proper credentials, take an oath of allegiance to the commonwealth, and enter into bond in the sum of £500; itinerant ministers were denied testimonials. This measure also validated marriages already solemnized by magistrates and others in the remote parts of the state.

The first important change in the Church of England during the Revolution was in the liturgy, as it had included prayers for the British royal family and acknowledgement of the authority of the King. On July 5, 1776, the Virginia Convention, which now held the reins of government in the province, resolved that such prayers should be omitted from the services. The twentieth and twenty-first sentences of the litany were also altered to include supplications to endow the magistrates of the commonwealth with "grace, wisdom, and understanding" and to give them "grace to execute justice, and to maintain truth."

At the end of the Revolution the Reverend David Griffith, minister of Christ Church, Alexandria, where Washington worshipped, lamented "the declining state of the Church of England" and the "pitiable situation of her clergy." Although he was convinced that the Church still had powerful friends to give it encouragement and support, he was astonished at the "indifference and indolence" of the Church and clergy, especially when he reflected on the assiduity of the leaders of other denominations "to increase their influence" and "by open attacks, and subtle machinations" to become preeminent.

Indeed, Griffith predicted that unless the clergy came up with "some well-regulated plan," the ruin of the Church was inevitable, even without the "malevolence of her enemies." Considering that the Church was "without ordination, without government, without support, unprotected by the laws, and yet labouring under injurious restriction from laws" still in effect, "her destruction" was certain unless corrective measures were adopted. Griffith thought that while the War was in progress "it would have been imprudent to enter on a regulation of ecclesiastical affairs," but now such reason no longer existed. What he proposed was a clerical convention to meet in Richmond to adopt remedial measures. The upshot was that in 1785 the Virginia legislature incorporated the Protestant Episcopal Church on petition of the clergy of that denomination.

The Presbyterians fared relatively well during the Revolution. They grew in number, established schools, helped to divest the Anglican Church of special privilege, and earned an unrivaled reputation for patriotism. There was nothing protean in their attitude toward the Revolution. Indeed, some Anglicans regarded them as "mere retailers of politics, sowers of sedition and rebellion." Their clergy, Cresswell charged, were "particularly active in supporting the measures of Congress from the Rostrum, gaining proselytes, persecuting the unbelivers, preaching up the righteousness of their cause and persuading the unthinking populace of the infallibility of success." At the rate they were gaining converts, some of these "religious rascals" were doubtless looking forward to establishing the Presbyterian faith over the entire continent. Nothing of the sort was contemplated, of course. But their success did elicit some jealousy.

The Baptists, too, were "in high spirits" during the Revolution, urging the disestablishment of the Anglican Church, gaining converts, pressing for liberalization of marriage laws, proposing that the overseers of the poor be elected by the community at large, and—in the eyes of the conservatives—being generally offensive. Their preachers, Dr. Honyman reported, were usually "mean, illiterate enthusiasts" and their crowded meetings were "terrible scenes of screaming, lamentations, convulsions" and the "wildest enthusiasm." Most of the time they preached in the woods and by the river, but a few of the old school Baptists, who had emigrated early from England and Wales, had meeting houses. Despite the derision heaped upon them, the Baptists saw their efforts crowned with success. For instance, a Virginia Baptist Association meeting in Cumberland in August 1775 proposed that marriage should be regarded as a civil contract between a man and a woman to live together in and to perform the duties of the marriage state; that it was no part of the ministerial office to marry persons; that public notice of the intention to marry should be made on three successive Sundays, in a place of public worship; and that after obtaining a certificate of this intention, the man and woman in the presence of witnesses should jointly and separately agree to enter into marriage.

Methodism, which continued as an evangelical movement within the Church of England until 1784, was under a cloud during the Revolution because its founder and spiritual head, John Wesley, was an avowed tory, and all of his missionaries except Francis Asbury returned to England early in the conflict. Moreover, the native American Methodist preachers displayed no martial ardor, but rather a muted pacifism that offended the whigs. Yet Philip Gatch was probably the only Methodist minister who was actually assaulted in Virginia. One day, while riding to his Sussex County Circuit appointment, he was seized by two men who twisted his arms so badly that his shoulders were bruised. A tarring which poor Gatch suffered in Maryland permanently injured one of his eyes.

In spite of tribulation, though, and a near-schism in 1770, the

Methodists in Virginia increased in number during the revolutionary years largely through the prudence and zeal of the itinerant preachers peerlessly led by Asbury. "I laboured with brother Hill," Asbury reported in May 1780 "I showed him the evil of a separation, which he seems to be afraid of. Our people's leaving the Episcopal Church has occasioned the people of that Church to withdraw from our preaching . . . . I advised our friends to attend the Episcopal Church, that prejudice might be removed; then their people will attend us . . . . "

Although at this time Asbury expected few hearers in the James River area, the following year Freeborn Garretson reported that crowds attended his own preaching. In the Fluvanna Circuit, Garretson even found that some people had emancipated their slaves. News of this must have pleased Asbury, who had spoken "to some select friends about slave-keeping, but they could not bear it . . . . " Asbury consoled himself with the thought that God would "plead the cause of the oppressed" though it gave offense to say so in Virginia. This kind of political and social restraint, coupled with intensified preaching, resulted in an increase in the followers; in 1779, of a total Methodist population of 8,577, 4,507 were in Virginia circuits.

Despite the step taken toward religious freedom during the Revolution, the war, with its attendant violence and lust for gain, sapped the spirituality of the people. As the Baptist historian, Robert Semple, put it, "the war, though very propitious to the liberty of the Baptists, had an opposite effect upon the life of religion, among them." Such was the case for the other denominations in Virginia whether or not they had suffered from the persecutions which, in the case of the Baptists, had really "been favourable to vital piety." With religious liberty came "leanness of soul" and indifference; attendance at religious meetings declined; "iniquity greatly abounded;" and the love of many "waxed cold." But not for long, for precisely this kind of soil provided the maximum challenge for the laborers in God's vineyard.

VI.

AFTER years of relative peace except for Indian forays in the West, Virginia felt the impact of war during the Revolution. Destructive raids battered Tidewater with increasing effectiveness and kept the inhabitants in a constant state of alarm. Slaves, livestock, fowls, grain, vegetables, fruit, fodder, household goods, and horses were taken from owners without apologies or promises of payment. In Virginia's far west, along the Ohio and its tributaries, the perpetual threat of Indian attack frequently materialized into bloody reality that annihilated entire families.

It was during these violent years that the women of Virginia learned that war "is indeed terrible," especially when brought to their very doors. Yet throughout the conflict they generally remained at home ministering to the needs of their households, assuming the responsibilities of many an absent husband, meeting as best they could the inevitable wartime scarcities, and coping with high prices. Salt, for instance, rose from 26 shillings in 1776 to £6 and £7 in 1778; calomel (much used for medication) from £3 per ounce in 1777 to £24 Virginia currency in 1778; a paper of pins from $1 in 1776 to twice that much the following year. Only when they faced the danger of personal violence or capture did the women of Virginia abandon their lares and penates for safety.

As if danger, privation, and loneliness were not enough, the Revolution brought destitution to some wives and to widows of men in the military service. Even before the Continental currency declined in value, soldiers' pay had not been uniform, prompt, or sufficient. Aware of this, in December 1776, the Virginia General Assembly resolved that in the event money from public subscription proved insufficient, the county courts be required to furnish wives and

53

children of poor soldiers with provisions to meet their needs. The following May an act for such purpose included aged parents; and in October assistance was extended to widows of men who had died or been killed in service. Two years later, in 1779, however, measures for the support of dependents were repealed on the ground that they had "created an expenditure greatly exceeding the expectations of the legislature. . . ."

Obviously the legislative intent was to restrict public support to the needy, and then only in the most meager measure. Little wonder, then, that enlistments lagged and desertions increased. Also skirting indigence were the widows and orphans of clergymen, whose economic situation had never been good, even before the disestablishment of the Church of England. In the absence of pensions and insurances, help for them could come only through church collections and parishioners' gifts.

In assuming many of the responsibilities of absent husbands, women had to cope with special problems. First of all, on some large plantations there was a manpower shortage resulting from losses of slaves and from a dearth of indentured servants. Then, as military needs for supplies increased, women had to fend off demands for foodstuffs, horses, and wagons from both friends and enemies.

Frances Bland Tucker was fortunate in having the guidance of her husband, St. George Tucker, when requisitioning was intensified during the Yorktown campaign. "You will *in case of a requisition*," he advised her on September 22, 1781, "direct the Overseer to deliver all that can possibly be spared, but do not order any to be delivered unless a requisition be made, as it is possible they may not want to collect Beef so high up the Country. . . ." The following day he told her to "temporize" with any public agent who might call to obtain supplies but not to display "in the smallest degree an aversion to parting with the fruits of the plantation to the public." His reason for counseling delay was that in a few days French agents were to be ordered out with hard money—the scarcest of media in Virginia—to purchase supplies for both the American and French armies. This information, Tucker cautioned, was to be kept secret, else it might have the disastrous effect of stopping collections then underway.

Even when their husbands remained at home, women suffered the vicissitudes of war. For instance, President Madison of the College of William and Mary and his wife were turned out of their house in Williamsburg in 1781 to provide quarters for Cornwallis and were even denied the use of their own well. Fortunately, they found shelter at the College, and they were young. Some women accustomed to servants were positively helpless without them. One who lost her cook was obliged to solicit her neighbors to prepare her food. And with the "plague of flies" left by the British when they evacuated the town, it was "impossible to eat, drink, sleep, write, sit still or even walk about in peace" much less to cook a palatable meal in the primitive kitchens of the day.

For the average housewife, though, life went on much as usual during the struggle for independence. The kitchen and garden continued to be her domain: she milked the cows, fed the chickens, hoed the vegetables, looked after the children, nursed her aged parents, prepared and cooked the food, washed and mended the clothing, and swept the house. At least she had little fear that an officer would requisition her cramped abode to accommodate the military.

On the score of toiletries and dress the woman of humble station was also less inconvenienced than her aristocratic sister. Prior to the Revolution ladies could purchase not only a variety of cloth, shoes, accessories, hair-pins, combs, brushes, buttons, tooth-brushes and powder, fragrant essences, face powder and puffs, and toys for the children—some of them items whose use was restricted to the wellborn. These gradually disappeared from the shops after the break with the chief supplier, England.

During the days of forced austerity, some women probably consulted such a practical manual as *The Accomplished Lady's Delight in Preserving, Physick, Beautifying, Cookery, and Gardening* . . , part one of which gave instructions for making facial unguents and powders, for preparing whiteners for the teeth and sweeteners of the breath and for curling hair. If no such useful aid was available, one needed only to apply to friends to learn about the efficacy of barley water, eggs, milk, and some plants to keep the skin soft, youthful, and free from blemishes. Having gone without cosmetics, the farm wife never bothered with such luxuries. If she wanted fragrance she thrust some "bubby-flower"—a sweet-scented shrub—into her bosom and entrusted her looks to nature.

Because the ladies were fired by patriotism, it became almost fashionable to abandon British extravagancies, to wear homemade clothing, and to have the hair dressed less elaborately than before. Mrs. William Byrd III of Westover cut up the curtains to make

Westover, Charles City County. Built about 1730 by Colonel William Byrd II.
Courtesy of Virginia State Library.

clothing and used the linings for underwear. As early as 1774 attention was given to insuring an adequate supply of wool, but not of cotton. But as imported sheeting and other cloth became increasingly scarce, the cultivation of cotton took on new importance, and a crude cotton gin was used for the first stage of processing the fiber. On large plantations, carding and spinning of cotton and wool became the chief employment of female blacks, some of whom learned to produce cloth "little inferior to that made in Manchester."

Since women could not fight, they were resolved to support the struggle for independence through industry, particularly in the production of clothing. "Let us," exhorted Anne Terrel of Bedford County, "in some measure, lay aside our visiting and fashions, and earnestly attend to carding, spinning, and weaving, and brown our fair arms in our bleach yards, and instead of the fine gewgaws of Great Britain wear linen of our own manufacturing; and although it may not be so very fine, yet we may say we paid nothing for it to Great Britain, and that we are free women, and while our dear husbands are nobly struggling in the army for that freedom, let us be fervent in prayer to ALMIGHTY GOD for their protection and safe return. . . ."

To encourage production, at least two manufacturies were established—one at Williamsburg and one at Fredericksburg—which employed slave and indentured labor. And all women, whether in mansion or cabin, clicked their knitting needles with intensity. Watching his wife at this work, Landon Carter made the computation that in the six days that it required her to make one stocking, she took 333,000 stitches!

During the Revolution opportunities for gainful employment continued to be meager, not that there were many women seeking such work. Some of the few who had kept shops had to close for lack of stock, since such luxuries as capers, olives, English crockery, pots, and pans virtually disappeared from the market. Shortly after the adoption of the Association, Jane Charlton advertised that there had just arrived in the "last" ships from London a "GENTEEL assortment of MILLINERY, LACES, Dresden SUITS, SILKS, JEWELRY, and sundry other articles, all in the newest fashion." During the War such items could enter Virginia through illicit trade only, unless they were of French manufacture. Tea was from the start mixed with the stigma of toryism, and coffee and sugar became increasingly scarce.

On the other hand, midwives were as busy as ever—a soldier's leave was generally fruitful—and there was an increased demand for nurses to attend the sick. One woman took over the management of a large tanning yard following the death of her husband. Another was employed as a jailer by Isle of Wight County. A few bold ladies, largely in fun, once assisted in making munitions. The clothing as well as the textile industry also provided a little work, though at exploitative wages. Early in 1781 at the height of the inflation, some women refused to make soldiers' shirts at the rate of fifteen dollars each, paid in certificates of doubtful value. No one wanted to work for nothing.

The worst ordeal that Virginia women had to face was having to flee from their homes. Even more unfortunate were those who lost their homes in the holocausts that virtually destroyed several coastal towns. Apprehending the danger to the exposed Norfolk area, the Buckingham County Committee of Safety in 1775 assured a refuge to the inhabitants of the lower counties, together with their slaves and livestock, in the event they should be driven from their homes.

This kindly gesture started a veritable contest among the inland counties of Virginia and continued into 1776 following the destruction of Norfolk, which reduced that bustling seaport to charred ruin. The Virginia Convention immediately voted £1,000 for the distressed inhabitants of the place and ordered the Committee of Safety to provide for their removal to the interior. The Sussex County Committee offered houses and land for as many "poor people" as could be accommodated; Mecklenburg County promised the refugees "a cordial reception"; and Amelia County proffered aid to the victims of the "cruel hand of oppression."

Meanwhile patriots from Princess Anne and Norfolk counties reported to the Convention that tory "ruffians" in their neighborhoods had "ravaged" their plantations, "stripped almost to nakedness" their wives and children, "invaded" their chambers "at the silent hour of midnight," and not only stolen plate, money, and everything of value, but also reduced houses to ashes. Such reports led wealthy Archibald Cary to send wagons eastward to help remove the people of these counties.

In the spring of 1779 opulent Virginia was the target of a British raid-in-force of 1,800 men commanded by Major General Edward Mathew. The invaders landed at Portsmouth and meeting little resistance captured Gosport, Kemp's Landing, and Suffolk, destroying every kind of property, including houses, furniture, a shipyard and ropewalk, naval stores, and merchandise. In one instance they even stooped to robbing four boys of their clothing, buckles, and money. "Struck with dread and consternation," many of the inhabitants fled carrying all that they could with them, but "the more cool and deliberate" resolved to remain in their homes and hope for the best. For some this was a mistake, for it was reported that the British troops' behavior toward women and children was "as unmanly as it was degrading & barbarous." One woman was plundered of her money, clothes, and most valuable furniture, and when stripped of her rings had the flesh of her fingers torn. At least three girls, it was said, one of whom was soon to be married, were forced on board the enemy ships. How many cases of rape occurred during the War is not known for the reason given in a Congressional report which stated that "such is the nature of that most irreparable injury, that the persons suffering it, and their relations, though perfectly innocent, look upon it as a kind of reproach to have the facts related, and their names known." Americans, though, had to admit that the British high command meted out "exemplary & rigorous justice" to troops found guilty of such offences. During the Cornwallis campaign, Dr. Honyman reported, two soldiers who had raped a nine-year-old girl were given one hour to prepare for death and then were hanged before the entire army. Although "acts of violence and rapine" inevitably occurred, the officers, who generally behaved with "moderation and civility," did what they could to redress them.

As early as 1779 Mrs. Frances Bland Tucker, mistress of Matoax, near Petersburg on the Prince George side of the Appomattox River, became alarmed by news of enemy movements, especially since her husband had recently joined a volunteer company and she was expecting her first child by him. Fortunately she had another plantation, Bizarre, in Cumberland County, where she planned to repair in the event the British remained around Portsmouth. To the relief of all Virginians, the enemy left.

But as 1780 drew to a close there arrived in Virginia waters the traitor Benedict Arnold, with a powerful flotilla that laid waste the James River area as far as Richmond. In January 1781, The Tuckers decided to move westward. The little cavalcade that left Matoax included an infant and its delicate mother (poor Frances was almost constantly pregnant); three sons by her former marriage; the Tucker's firstborn (a little girl); Maria Rind (whose mother had briefly been printer of *The Virginia Gazette*); Miss Patty Hall; and the house servants. There was also some furniture. It took them some days to cover the fifty miles of muddy road between Matoax and Bizarre, a much less spacious place than the recently evacuated plantation. As soon as his family was settled in their cramped new quarters, St. George joined a company of volunteers ordered southward to aid General Nathanael Greene. Frances tried to make the best of things in the "smoky cabin" that needed repair. After Tucker's discharge following the battle of Guilford Court House, he rejoined his family in April 1781. But not for long. With the approach of summer the military situation became so alarming that St. George, now a lieutenant colonel with Virginia forces under Baron von Steuben, sent urgent word to his wife to lose no time in moving the family to Roanoke plantation, forty miles from Bizarre; their stay there way brief. By July they were "well and happy" at Bizarre. And there they stayed until hostilities came to a close.

Even young girls without family responsibilities found displacement "one of the calamities" of their lives. Such, at least, was the opinion of Betsy Ambler, who moved from York to Richmond and then to a cottage farther west. When the British raided the little Virginia capital in 1781, she wrote her friend Mildred Smith: "We were off in a twinkling. . . . Such terror and confusion you have no idea of—Governor, counsel every body scampering. . . ." Since Betsy's father held the office of treasurer in the Virginia government and thus was a prime target for the enemy, he hid at night in an old coach faithfully guarded by a trusted slave. One evening, just as he had been committed to "his solitary confinement" and the family sat down to a "frugal supper," a party of Virginia militia knocked on the door to give notice that the enemy were on their way, but where the enemy was specifically, was not known. A quick consultation followed and then flight through "by ways and brambles" until they reached the main road to Charlottesville, their destination being a plantation nearby, where they hoped to find a bed. When they arrived there they found the place empty. They were about to spread their pallets on the floor when they received word that the dreaded scourge, Colonel Banastre Tarleton, was approaching. In a state of near-panic they retraced their steps to the self-same spot they had left the night before.

These were far from being isolated cases in 1781. Dr. Honyman found that slaves were flocking to the British, and on some plantations not one remained. People were frantically moving their blacks, cattle, horses, saddles, bridles, and other possessions out of reach of the enemy; the "hardships, distress & damage" were "unspeakable." Not knowing where the British might appear next, many Virginians were fleeing from the Richmond-Fredericksburg area westward to Albemarle County. General Nelson, for one, was "sending off his family with great expedition." The inhabitants who remained within reach of the enemy were "under the greatest terror imaginable" owing to the rumors they had heard of "the inhuman ravages and cruelties of the British troops." Although experience eventually showed that these were exaggerated rumors, many persons still buried their most valuable effects and took to the woods and thickets rather than risk an encounter with the enemy. Actually Cornwallis and his aides "behaved with the greatest politeness" toward their reluctant hosts or hostesses when they lodged at plantation houses along their route, but the troops brought devastation to the outlying premises. At Mrs. Nicholas's, for example, they killed much livestock and poultry and either consumed or wasted 150 barrels of corn; and the stench from offal and putrefying animal flesh was almost unbearable. Since the men had no tents, they stretched out under temporary sheds or arbors made with boughs of trees and fence rails.

In the transmontane region conditions worsened after 1777, when the emboldened Indians intensified their attacks along Virginia's extended frontier and raided as far eastward as the Greenbriar Valley. Scornful of danger, some settlers were averse to abandoning their homes even after the furtive tap of a scout at the cabin door or window warned them to escape to a fort; indeed, for a few the very thought of moving was nearly "as bad as Deth." Yet time and again there was no alternative except to dash to the crowded shelter of the stockade with its primitive sanitary facilities. In 1777 the "poor Kentucky people" reported that for some time they had been confined to three forts which the Indians had tried to reduce several times. The savages had taken most of their horses, burned their corn, and left them with only a two-month supply of bread and no means of relieving the destitution of the refugees, among whom were nearly two hundred women and children.

Forting, slaughter, and capture continued south of the Ohio with ominous regularity. "We are all Obliged to live in forts . . . ," John Floyd reported to Governor Jefferson from Kentucky on April 16, 1781, "and notwithstanding all the Caution that we use, forty seven of the Inhabitants have been Killed and Taken by the Savages Besides a number Wounded, since the first of Jany." Whole families had been annihilated without regard to age or sex and infants torn from their mothers' arms "and their Brains dashed out against Trees." Casualties among the men had been so great that there were now many "helpless indigent Widows and Orphans." In Jefferson County the Indians had killed or captured more than forty women and children in the space of two months.

In times of danger women were no whit less courageous and resourceful than men. During the first siege of Fort Henry at Wheeling in 1777 women moulded bullets in frying pans, made linen bandages, and occasionally filled gaps in the firing line. When the place was set on fire, they carried tubs of water to drench the flaming roofs. In September 1782 the Indians again attacked Fort Henry. Before the Indians arrived the defenders, alerted by scouts, carried into the fort some of the powder that had been stored in the nearby house of Colonel Ebenezer Zane who, with a few companions and two servants, remained with the rest of the military stores. The persistent assaults of the savages so depleted the supply of powder in the fort that it became necessary to replenish it from the magazine at Colonel Zane's. Among the volunteers to make the hazardous dash for powder was young Elizabeth Zane, sister of the Colonel. "You have no men to spare," she is said to have told the commander of the fort, Captain Silas Zane, also her brother, "and a woman will not be missed in defending the fort." The intrepid girl had her way, and miraculously accomplished the mission without receiving a scratch, although legend has it that a bullet hole was found in her dress.

Yet war was not all privation and danger; for some women it actually had a rare, exciting side which they probably remembered long after its somber and hazardous aspects were forgotten. For one thing, the Revolution brought to Virginia the French troops with their colorful uniforms, their verve, and their remarkable appreciation of feminine charm. "There is something so flattering in the [att]entions of these elegant french officers, and tho' not one in ten of them can speak a word of English, yet their style of entertaining and their devotion to the Ladies of Yk. is so flattering that almost any girl of 16 would be enchanted." On their part the ladies showered the Gallic allies with hospitality. Thus the French had an opportunity to learn how attractive ("though not particularly pretty") and "fond of laughter" the ladies were, how well they played musical instruments, and how they did "not lead," but rather "inspired a taste" for the chase; clever women that they were "they knew how to defend themselves from the hunters, but did not crush with their arrows those who dared look at them."

Although Virginia husbands may have lacked the suavity of the French, they had their own special ways of paying homage to the women. One was to call their wives "honey," which the French interpreted as "*mon petit coeur.*" Another was to pen verses, which were sometimes printed in the newspapers.

On the other hand, husbands sometimes beat their wives, and such indignity the poor women had to endure unless they had friends to whom they could turn or the courage to have their mates bound to keep the peace, in which case the husband had to give security for his good behavior.

Since personal counseling services and domestic relations courts were nonexistent, romantic and marital rifts and frustrations were occasionally aired in the press under gossamer anonymity. For instance, a jilted suitor of "Miss B---y R---ts, in Nansemond, near Milner's "informed her through this medium that "no woman is capable of being beautiful, who is not incapable of being false." When John Wright paraded his broken heart in *The Virginia Gazette*, his target took him to task: "None but the base and malevolent take pitiful advantages of the objects of their displeasure."

In the absence of a general divorce law, however, there was some justification for the public exposure of a broken marriage and for notification in the press that the husband would no longer be responsible for his wife's debts. Benjamin Bannerman, for example, accused his wife of having tried to poison him and of running up a huge debt for him after they had decided to live apart, thus obliging him to stop her credit.

When a Virginia woman married, "her legal existence was suspended or incorporated into that of her husband," who not only came into possession of her personal property and a life estate in her lands, but also took any other income that might be hers. Single women, and that included widows, could sue and be sued, enter into contracts, execute deeds, dispose of their estates by will, administer the estates of deceased husbands, and serve as guardians of minors. But all women—wives, widows, and spinsters—were denied participation in politics. Mrs. Hannah Corbin sounded a faint note of women's liberation when she wrote her brother, Richard Henry Lee, that widows should not be taxed for the property they controlled, since women did not have the right to vote. Liberal-minded Lee raised no objection to this extreme proposal, but pointed out that taxes levied by the representatives of the people applied to themselves as well as to their constituents.

In at least one respect, though, the ideology of the Revolution brought little change of feminine mind. As the astute Schoepf put it: "No matter if . . . in general equality of all ranks is promoted and defended, the ladies here are not the more inclined to part with any advantage of position to which they fancy themselves entitled through the offices held by their husbands." In Richmond news of the definitive treaty of peace was the occasion for illuminations, fireworks, banquets, and, of course, a ball at which the honor of the first dance fell by lot to the daughter of a shoemaker. That this distinction should be left to chance displeased the ladies of the Governor's family and others. But public opinion held "that the lot should be valid as against any claims of rank, and that no exception to the generally allowed equality should be granted even the fair sex beyond that due personal merit and accomplishment."

In the unobtrusive eighteenth-century way, the Virginia women of '76 conducted themselves with remarkable fortitude during the long years of war. Forced to cope with niggardly dependent assistance, scarcities and high prices, shortage of help, incursions of the enemy, and finally invasion, the women muted their complaints and managed to feed and clothe their families, to render volunteer services, and even to stimulate patriotic ardor. Probably the report that in Amelia County the young ladies had entered into an agreement not to permit "the addresses of any person," unless he had served in the American forces long enough to prove "by his valour" that he was deserving of their love was the fabrication of some romantic mind. And perhaps there was no truth in the story that Mrs. Lucy Gilmer "with tearful eyes" proffered her jewels to Jefferson and "asked him to use them in the cause of her country." But doubtless many women emulated the "Spartan mother" during the struggle for independence.

VI.

"WAR never fails to injure the morals of the people engaged in it. The American War, in particular, had an unhappy influence of this kind. Being begun without funds or regular establishments, it could not be carried on without violating private rights; and in its progress it involved a necessity for breaking solemn promises and plighted public faith." So observed Dr. David Ramsay, and what he said about the country as a whole applied to Virginia. During the War for Independence, Virginia, like other states, was inundated with paper money to meet the extraordinary expenses occasioned by the struggle. So abundant was the supply of this money of continental and state issue that by 1779 it was circulating at 45 to 1 of specie; a year later the market rate was 50 to 1; in early spring of 1781 it was 100 to 1; in July it was 600 to 1; and by September it was 1,000 to 1.

Prices already sensitive to political and military developments, to seasonal changes, to crop yields, and to volume of imports chiefly from the French and Dutch West Indies, rose in proportion to the declining value of paper to which were added quantities of counterfeit bills. Even the inoculation law of 1777 affected the price of calomel. Fortunately, the scarcity of salt, an indispensable commodity (Landon Carter estimated that his kitchen alone used three quarts a week), was eased by importations and, to a much less extent, by successful experiments for extracting it from river and bay water. Still, its price advanced at impressive pace: in mid-1776 it was 26 shillings a bushel; it then fell to 12 shillings because of the several small vessels from Bermuda; the following year, 1777, it advanced to £4 in September, £7 in November, and £10 in December. In 1778 there was a price drop, but by April 1779 salt again sold for £10. By December 1780 the price had risen to £100 and in July 1781 to as high as £1500. Other commodities generally followed suit, reported Dr. Honyman. In April 1781 sugar brought $45 a pound; a saddle, £1500; a pair of shoes, $1,000. An average dinner at a tavern in early 1780 cost $20. No wonder people resorted to barter—a bushel of salt for a bushel of corn, or two gallons of spirits for a barrel of corn. With prices of necessaries so "monstrously enhanced," the poor, of course, suffered.

Initially it was a mark of Whiggism to accept the fiat money. In April 1777 when there was a rumor (started by a political opponent) that Richard Henry Lee was requiring his tenants to pay in sterling rather than paper, Landon Carter felt that Lee's public character had been "Stained by it." By 1778 though, everyone was so "totally engrossed with schemes & projects for making money that every other consideration [held] but an inferior place. Never were people so entirely infatuated by the rage of amassing. . . ." They bought, sold and invested with the enthusiasm of brokers. One of the favorite forms of investment was in land, whose price rose less than anything else during the War because there was plenty of it. At the end of 1779 it generally sold at twenty times its former value, whereas other forms of property, such as Negroes, sold "at astonishing rates." Many holders of unredeemed certificates received in payment for commodities sold to the government took them to land offices to exchange them for land warrants. These, at the selling price of land, were even more advantageous than specie certificates honored by the treasury, since the latter were paid at the official instead of the market rate of exchange. The resulting heavy emigration to the western part of the state was only temporarily checked by Indian forays.

Debtors, of course, took advantage of the monetary anarchy to pay their debts, but the tender law of 1777 did not absolutely oblige creditors to accept payment in paper money; if it was tendered and refused, however, interest on the debt was extinguished. Since refusal could lay one open to the charge of disaffection, many creditors reluctantly accepted paper when the exchange rate was no more than 20 and 25 for one. On the receipt of paper the prudent man rushed to invest it in land, slaves, tobacco, or other property. Real estate in Richmond following the city's designation as the state capital attracted speculation. With the repeal of the 1777 tender law in November 1781, the circulation of paper money stopped, despite the fact that there was very little specie in Virginia. The only alternative for merchants stocked with imports from New England and the West

Indies, which began to be plentiful by the end of 1781, was to extend credit, and this they did, at the same time charging extravagant prices. Such was not the case with country produce, now that the demand for it had diminished with the departure of the bulk of the armed forces.

Although the price rise in Virginia was typical of what was happening in other parts of the country, the Old Dominion did not attempt to impose elaborate and unworkable wage and price controls as did the New England states. To be sure, half-hearted attempts at price regulation were made at Williamsburg and York, but nothing came of them. Virginia's avoidance of economic controls appears all the more remarkable when one considers that it had to meet not only local demands, but also those on the Convention troops interned in the state and, in 1781, those of both allied and enemy armies. On both sides the waste of foodstuffs, not unusual among armed forces, was almost as great as the consumption. After the surrender at Yorktown, Dr. Honyman noted that two thousand cattle were left to perish by the departing troops. Another not inconsiderable factor in the price situation toward the end of the War was the cornering of goods by wholesalers—"speculators"—who retailed them at enormous rates.

In face of the Pandora's box opened by the War, the martial spirit began to ebb even before the adoption of the Declaration of Independence, as evidenced by the difficulties in filling the ranks and by the advertisements for deserters. The responses which appeared to a few of these advertisements were of course exculpatory. One deserter pled that he was ill, another that he had enlisted without parental consent, another that he had hired a substitute. An so it went.

Desertions doubtless would have been checked had the punishment for such offense been more severe. Even Washington was obliged to use lenity in dealing with the problem. But there was no stopping the runaways, who either skulked at home or made off to the south or the back country on the Ohio. Of twenty-seven men drafted from Hanover County in 1777, Dr. Honyman reported, twenty deserted.

In spite of increasing emoluments in the form of bounties for military service, Virginians continued to display some reluctance to serve in either the Continental Army or the state militia. Many hired substitutes by paying them considerable sums above the bounties offered by the state, although these were substantial and allowed for the declining value of the currency. The militia law of May 1780 provided for pay ranging from 125 pounds of tobacco and ten rations per day for a brigadier general to 7½ pounds of tobacco and one ration for a private. Yet, according to Dr. Honyman, many of the men recruited marched southward "very unwillingly," and in several counties there were "violent mutinies." The May 1780 act for recruiting Virginia's quota for the Continental Army provided for individual bounties of 1,000 pounds of tobacco. In October additional bounties were offered to encourage enlistments: $12,000 to each recruit for the duration of the war and $8,000 to each recruit for three years' enlistment. Moreover, men who served for the duration of the War were to receive a "healthy sound negro, between the ages of ten and thirty years," or £60 in specie at the option of the soldier; finally, each soldier would be entitled to 300 acres of land in lieu of all bounties provided by former laws.

As early as 1777 Governor Patrick Henry obliquely acknowledged the tepid martial spirit by requiring recruiting officers to encourage enlistments and by recommending to the clergy of all denominations "to exert in their several Stations their influence for effecting so salutary a purpose." He especially relied on the Presbyterians, who, as Dr. Honyman put it, had "always been furious" in the patriot cause. By early 1779 scarcities, high prices, and military setbacks were producing an unabashed desire for peace. "Surely," people were saying, "no country ever wanted that blessing so much as this miserable impoverished ruined land." By mid-year their hopes had risen, and they were betting that they would have peace by Christmas, since rumor had it that the British would offer independence to the Americans if they renounced the French alliance. But instead of peace, the Virginians were to experience in the next two years all the calamities of war.

At the end of hostilities, Virginians were complaining of great "depravity" and "corruption of manners" among all ranks of people. Morality was "at a very low ebb, & religion almost extinguished." People were recklessly going into debt and condoning doubtful financial practices. To make matters worse, they even lost respect for the chief magistrates: Governor Jefferson and the Council because of their "neglect" and "supineness" during Arnold's invasion; and Governor Nelson because of his impressment policy.

If social life in Virginia was not purified in the crucible of the War for Independence, if, indeed—as David Ramsay said of the entire country—the old-fashioned moral character was "inferior to what it formerly was," Virginia emerged from the conflict with certain social gains. These derived from the enlightened, far-reaching revision of the laws, toward which George Mason, Edmund Pendleton, George Wythe, Thomas Jefferson, James Madison, and other made such conspicuous contributions.

A Note on the Sources

THE primary sources for a study of social life in Virginia during the War for Independence are abundant and varied. An especially important manuscript is the Diary of Robert Honyman, M. D. (Library of Congress), which contains a wealth of data on economic trends during this period. Also of substantial value are the Tucker-Coleman Papers (Earl G. Swem Library) and the Eliza Jaquelin Ambler Papers (Colonial Williamsburg). The Draper Manuscripts (Wisconsin Historical Society), many of which were edited by Reuben G. Thwaites and Louise P. Kellogg and published by the Society, provide a detailed account of events in the West.

Indispensable for any study of eighteenth-century Virginia is *The Virginia Gazette*, whose use if facilitated by the index prepared by Lester J. Cappon and Stella F. Duff (Williamsburg, 1950).

To supplement printed official documents there are collections of letters of eminent Virginians, among them Thomas Jefferson, George Washington, and Richard Henry Lee. Jefferson's only book, *Notes on the State of Virginia* (William Peden ed., Chapel Hill, 1955), is a quasi-official work touching on a number of subjects. Letters, diaries, and proceedings are also included in the issues of *The Virginia Magazine of History and Biography* and *The William and Mary Quarterly*.

Journals and reminiscences afford information on all aspects of Virginia society. Especially valuable are: *The Diary of Landon Carter of Sabine Hall, 1752-1778* (Jack P. Greene ed., Charlottesville, 1965); Joseph Doddridge, *Notes on the Settlement and Indian Wars* (Parsons, W. Va., 1960); *Journal & Letters of Philip Vickers Fithian, 1773-1774* (Hunter D. Farish ed., Williamsburg, 1957); *Philip Vickers Fithian: Journal, 1775-1776* (Robert G. Albion, Leonidas Dodson eds., Princeton, 1934); *The Journal of John Harrower, An Indentured Servant in the*

Colony of Virginia, 1773-1776 (Edward M. Riley ed., New York, 1963); (Lucinda Lee Orr), *Journal of a Young Lady of Virginia* (Baltimore, 1871).

Travelers in Virginia during the Revolution left vivid records of their experiences. The most important of these are: Thomas Anburey, *Travels Through the Interior Parts of America* (2 vols., London, 1789); Marquis de Chastellux, *Travels in North America* (Howard C. Rice, Jr., ed., 2 vols., Chapel Hill, 1963); *The Journal of Nicholas Cresswell 1774-1777* (New York, 1924); *Baroness von Riedesel and the American Revolution* (Marvin L. Brown, Jr., trans. and ed., Chapel Hill, 1965); Johann D. Schoepf, *Travels in the Confederation* (New York, 1968); *The Revolutionary Journal of Baron von Closen 1780-1783* (Evelyn M. Acomb trans. and ed., Chapel Hill. 1958).

The basic secondary work on Virginia's social history is Mary Newton Stanard *Colonial Virginia, Its People and Customs* (Philadelphia, 1917). There are also specialized studies of great value such as: Wyndham B. Blanton, *Medicine in Virginia in the Eighteenth Century* (Richmond, 1931); Julia Cherry Spruill, *Women's Life and Work in the Southern Colonies* (Chapel Hill, 1938); James Curtis Ballagh, *A History of Slavery in Virginia* (Baltimore, 1902); Benjamin Quarles, *The Negro in the American Revolution* (Chapel Hill, 1961). Two venerable studies of religion in Virginia are those of Robert B. Semple, *A History of the Rise and Progress of the Baptists in Virginia* (Richmond, 1810) and Bishop William Meade, *Old Churches, Ministers and Families of Virginia* (2 vols., Philadelphia, n.d.). Also important are William Warren Sweet's *Religion on the American Frontier, The Baptists 1783-1830* (New York, 1931); *Methodism in American History* (Nashville, 1961); and *Virginia Methodism* (Richmond, 1955). And there is the politically oriented work of H. J. Eckenrode, *The Revolution in Virginia* (Boston and New York, 1916).